BUILT TO GROW

THE GYM OWNER'S GUIDE TO SUCCESS AND SCALABILITY

TIM LYONS

BUILT TO GROW

Ordering Information: Quantity sales. Special discounts are available on quantity purchases by corporations, associations, and others. Orders by U.S. trade bookstores and wholesalers.
Please contact Tim Lyons
admin@pfmarketingsolutions.com
Or visit www.pfmarketingsolutions.com for more information about his company ProFit Marketing Solutions

DREAMSTARTERS

www.DreamStartersPublishing.com

Table of Contents

Introduction

This is a book for the Gym Owner, Fitness Director, or the Personal Trainer looking to start their own dream. This is for the leader of the team, the entrepreneur, the risk taker; you are the true leaders, the heroes of the fitness industry.

This book is about my story, but like many others, my challenges aren't unique. They are the same challenges that you may be finding in your business right now, or maybe you haven't hit them yet, and this book will help you make decisions. I've already made the mistakes so that you don't have to, and that is the real value you will find within the pages ahead.

The Fitness Industry is a special place, and most people are in this industry for the right reasons, and that is to change as many lives, as they can, for the better. This book is my way to do the same thing. If I can help you create a longer lasting, scalable business, that means more lives will change for the better through you, then, I did my part.

Helping change lives is a noble cause, but never forget that this is a business, and for you to be able to do your great work, you will need to stay in business. You can only do that by making money, and I hope you want to make as much money as possible doing what you love. Built to Grow will help you do just that. Make More Money.

The gym business can be great, but so many owners struggle, and I think it's because you just haven't been taught everything you need to know, I want to change that right now.

Thank you for picking this book up and giving it a read. I'd like to hear from you, as to what you thought about it and how it has helped you grow your business.

Remember, I am on your side, and your success is my success. Enjoy the ride, see you on the inside!

Chapter 1

What Kind of Business Do You Want?

I'm a Gym Owner, but I'm also a Fitness Marketer. A lot of people come to me for my advice because of that, because I'm in the industry, just like you are. In today's environment, I see so many newly-crowned "marketers" with little if any experience. They don't really understand our industry, which is very different from most other types of businesses, which creates a lot of trial and error. This book is for gym owners who need help marketing and want to get that help from a gym owner just like them.

Not from someone who has never been in the gym business, not from someone who USED to own a gym, but from someone who is right there with you, right now.

I know what you need. I understand the day-to-day challenges you are facing. I've been there, from starting from zero, experiencing massive growth and to expanding into a much larger facility. I've developed business and marketing strategies that have built the type of business that I wanted to create. Using this book, you can leverage my lessons and create the same thing for yourself. You can take your business where you want to take it, but only if you are willing work hard, work smart, and allow yourself to be guided through the process. You don't have to reinvent the wheel, I've already done that for you. Now it's your turn.

Think of me as your coach. As someone who's played the game and is still in the game. We will go over key marketing strategies, specific for gyms. You will also learn how to leverage your time so that you can grow your business from within. In order to get started, I think it's important to first define what kind of business you want to build. Asking yourself that question, before anything else, will then direct any action you take.

When I think about how I started to figure this out, I can go back to the time that my dad gave me the book, *Rich Dad, Poor Dad*, by Robert Kiyosaki, back in 1997. At the time, my dad was a Business

Owner. In fact, he was always a Business Owner when I was growing up. He mainly worked as a Consultant in the Telecommunications Industry, designing phone and security systems for major hotels across the world. With that being said, I grew up in an entrepreneurial household and that shaped my thinking from an early age.

That book he gave me has changed a lot of people's lives, but it wasn't that exact book that changed my mind and perspective about what I really wanted. Kiyosaki's book talked about "assets and expenses," the concept of money, and how to create wealth. Kiyosaki's book shares his story and lessons as to what the "rich" do compared to what the "poor" do.

That was great, but not really life-changing for me, but it opened my eyes to another book that Robert Kiyosaki wrote. *Rich Dad's Cash Flow Quadrant*. This book really put things in perspective for me. I now looked at the world around me, including my friends and my parents, in a different way. I would try to figure out, "what quadrant were they in?" If you're not familiar with the book, it basically breaks down everyone into one of four quadrants:

Employee

"You have a job"

Self-Employed

"You own a job"

Business Owner

"You own a system that works for you"

Investor

"Your money works for you"

Let's take a look at each of these more closely.

Employee

An Employee is somebody that works for somebody else. They punch a time clock, or maybe they're on salary, but they put their time in for a paycheck. There are a lot of people who make a great living being an employee, with much success, so there's no shame here.

Personally, and this is a very personal perspective, this just wasn't for me, and not what I wanted to do or be.

Self-Employed

Here, you have a job, but you are working for yourself. So, even though you are not working for someone else, you are still putting in the time to get paid, and your amount of pay is directly related to how much time you put in.

A lot of people think that by working in their own business they're considered a Business Owner, but that's really not true. In this quadrant, if you are self-employed, it means that you have to be directly involved in the business for it to generate revenue or profit. While a lot of gym owners that I work with think they're business owners, they're really self-employed. They do own their job, but without them being involved in the day-to-day operations of the business, the business can't sustain itself. The majority of the readers of this book will be in this quadrant.

Business Owner

This individual truly owns a business, with a business that runs on systems, and the systems run the business. The true Business Owner is not involved in the day-to-day operations of the business for it to generate revenue and profit. So, here you own a system and people work with you or for you to execute the system that generates money for you.

When I read about this quadrant in Kiyosaki's book, I realized that that's exactly where I wanted to be, the Business Owner. Every business decision I made was to create systems to own a business that didn't own me. Every action I took, to build my business, was to push myself to that top-right quadrant. I needed to build a business, and not own a job.

The lessons that we discuss in this book will help you to become a true Business Owner.

Investor

This book is not about this quadrant, but let's touch on it a little bit, as it may be a place you want to go in the future.

An investor is using money to make money. This is a way to generate revenue and profit by investing in other businesses, products and/or services. You can also invest in stocks, mutual funds, and using money to make more money.

This is my ultimate goal, but I'm not there, yet. Obviously, I have some investments, but I'm a Business Owner for the gym, and Self-Employed for the marketing and coaching aspect of my work until I can develop that business into a systems-based business.

At this point in my life, my gym truly is a business. I maybe work on it four hours a week. I've got a great team, and the business generates a seven-figure revenue. The business is successful, and it is an asset for me. I opened the business in 2009, and it took me six solid years to get it to where I wanted it because I was starting from nothing.

My path to opening my business wasn't the way most people start their gyms. In fact, I wasn't a

Personal Trainer at all. I was actually working in construction and had a friend who owned a gym in the town that I was living in at the time. His main job was as a police officer, and he was an absentee owner of this gym. My friend had a great facility where people would swipe their key fob, work out, and he would collect his check.

Back in 2006 when I met him, I saw that and thought, "Man, this is an easy business." I love fitness and had a background of athletics. I played college football and sports my whole life. I knew fitness and was trained by some great Strength & Conditioning Coaches in my day, and I thought, "What the heck! If he can do it, it's got to be something I can do."

Reading *Rich Dad's Cash Flow Quadrant* had pushed me into learning how to build a business that wasn't dependent on me. A business that I didn't need to be involved in directly for it to generate revenue. That one book I read so many years ago still guides the decisions around the businesses that I am involved in.

When I first started the gym in 2009, I did everything, myself. This is definitely not unusual and isn't something you should feel bad about if you find yourself in the same position. Most people have to do everything; you have to do the marketing, you have to train clients, you have to be a janitor and do all the sales. I wasn't afraid to do the work, and usually, that work on a business pays off in a big way. So, I didn't mind doing everything, but the challenge with that is, I was doing everything, I couldn't leverage myself enough to grow after the initial start up period. It's the difference between working in a business and working on the business.

Later on, around 2011, I strategically started hiring specific positions to replace the tasks I was personally doing in the business. I was hiring skill sets that I wasn't the best at, but also to free up my time. With the free time, my focus shifted directly to learning and implementing marketing for the business. I spent nearly all my time in finding, creating and testing marketing strategies at the gym. There wasn't much available for gyms at the time, everything was low tech, hard to track and was ineffective at best. I had to learn or create everything myself and this is where I developed my marketing foundation that has carried me through today.

My Dad still gives me books to read. I think he knows that by giving me this information he can help me solve any problem I may be facing immediately through knowledge. Now he's giving books to my daughter to read. He was a huge influence, not just for giving me the right books at the right time, but for modelling a type of life that gave me more opportunities than I might have seen otherwise. I really owe everything to my Dad, Tim Lyons Sr.

Exercise

Where are you now in the cash-flow quadrant?

_____

Where would you like to be in three years?

_____

_____

_____

_____

_____

Where would you like to be in 10 years?

_____

_____

_____

_____

_____

What steps do you need to take to help you reach your three-year goals?

_____

_____

_____

What steps do you think you need to reach your 10-year goals?

_____

_____

_____

"The resistance that you fight physically in the gym and the resistance that you fight in life can only build a strong character."

Arnold Schwarzenegger

Chapter 2

WORK- Be All In!

I didn't wake up one day, working in the fitness industry owning a gym. My travels to this business started when I worked in the construction industry. I played football in college, got a full-ride scholarship, and went to school to get a degree in Civil Engineering. Unfortunately, my college didn't have that degree, so I enrolled in the Construction Business Management Program. It was the closest thing I could find to Engineering. This worked out to be a great thing, because the degree was more a blue collar, hard work type of degree, which was right up my alley.

When I finished school, I was able to get an amazing opportunity with a commercial construction company in beautiful Newport Beach, California. I was loving life. I basically had the ocean right outside my door, and had a job pertinent to my degree within weeks after graduating, and stayed in the industry for over seven years until things changed.

In the construction management game, you start at the bottom. You're opening gates at four in the morning for the concrete guys, and you're locking things up at 10:00 p.m. when the finishers are done. You're THAT guy. Which was fine with me, because I knew I had to put the work in to get where I wanted to be. My goal was to be a Project Manager, or a General Manager of a division. I knew that if I put the work in, the reward was there. The work involved up to 90 hours a week, so I could work my way up in the company. I'm hard wired to work and I'm not afraid to put in the time.

Then something happened. In 2008, as most people know, there was a change in the economy. There was a massive economic crash; people were losing their jobs, their homes. Large financial houses were closing their doors. A bit of panic was in the air as the housing market crashed. I was caught in the middle of it, like so many others, in one of the most volatile industries - construction. Massive layoffs were happening, and the writing was on the wall. Nobody was keeping their job, at least not anyone at my level.

Fortunately, I had saved some money, and I already had drafted plans for the gym. In fact, we were already building it. My goal at the time was to keep my construction job and have my gym as a business on the side, a "side hustle." But, when 2008 happened, I was just thrown out onto the streets. The construction company where I worked originally had around 100 employees, and at the end of the layoffs there were only three employees left; the two owners and a secretary. It was that bad.

That layoff is what propelled me into the gym business prematurely, and I had to go "all-in." I had lost my job, and I knew I had to get things together. At the time, my wife was working, but we certainly couldn't afford to live on one income. There really wasn't any other option. If I was going to make the gm work, for me and my family, I had to absolutely go "all-in." It wasn't an option, there was no back-up plan.

That meant working from opening to close, taking sales appointments on Sundays, running errands, whatever it took to get the business up and off the ground, running and operating, I did it. Because of my background and my work ethic, this wasn't even anything that I questioned or complained about. I just knew I had to get my ass up and be there at 4:30 a.m., unlocking doors, training the last client at 9:00 p.m., then do it again the next day. It's just what I knew I was going to have to do, and I did it.

Relatively early on I saw how effective this effort was. When the gym opened, there were zero clients. By the end of the year, we had 200 clients. We stayed at that level for several years, but we went along, we changed our offerings, and our pricing increased over time, so our income was increasing. At the end of each month, I would see growth in the business, and fortunately we never slid backwards.

Then a funny thing happened. As we grew our revenue, our profits were dropping. I had hired employees who could help me reach the true Business Owner status I wanted. More employees meant higher overhead, and less profit but this was all part of the strategy. As these employees took us to a higher level, about five years into the business, we grew out of the initial space, and we moved into our current space which is more than double the size. We grew so fast and we were busting at the seams, we actually moved some workouts into the parking lot, we just didn't have any more room, and people were still coming.

My work-ethic propelled the business to grow rapidly, and it meant long hours, seven days a week, and no complaining. Today, unfortunately, I see the opposite attitude, especially from the younger generations coming through, who are trying to build a business. An attitude that just doesn't want to work or be tied to anything, with no work ethic. The attitude seems as if they want to have everything without working for it, almost like it's deserved or owed to them. It's sad, and I have to wonder if this attitude and mindset is being taught. I know there are people out there that have made millions of dollars from a startup without doing much of anything, especially when they fall into the right situation. It's not normal, but these stories seem to cloud the minds of too many, and they think that it will happen to them too. It's unfortunate.

Ronnie Coleman, the winner of the Mr. Olympia bodybuilding title for eight years in a row, is considered by most to be the greatest bodybuilder of all time. He was massive. He was strong. He worked his ass off in the gym, and he was winning competition after competition after competition. I followed his career, closely. Although he is thought of as a nice, humble guy, he was also extremely proud of his Mr. Olympia titles, which meant more to him than other Olympia winners because he was all-in on it, he knew nothing else, no back up plan.

The toll that body building takes on the body, and being a big massive guy like Ronnie Coleman, is intense. Today, Ronnie has sustained life-changing injuries. He is either walking with crutches or is in a wheelchair 90% of the time. As of the writing of this book, he is on his tenth back surgery to fix collapsed disks, including fusions and plates and screws. Even though he is in extreme pain and definitely against doctor's orders, Ronnie keeps working out. Ronnie has broken the screws off, continuing to train every day because he doesn't know a different life. At 55 years old and banged up, he still gets up at every morning at 4:30 a.m. to go to the gym and train. He actually has a key to the gym, and even though it's not his own gym, he opens it up, and starts getting after it long before anyone else is there.

One of the things that Ronnie is well known for is being a powerful and strong body-builder. He is considered the strongest Mr. Olympia of all time, including an 800 lbs. back squat, for two reps. Much later down the line, the story goes that he was laid up in the hospital bed, for his sixth or seventh surgery, and he couldn't walk. A reporter, interviewing him, asks, "You're one of the greatest bodybuilders of all time, you've won eight Mr. Olympia titles, and now you can't walk, you're a broken man. Do you have any regrets, do you think this was all worth it to you?" Ronnie answers, "You know what? I do have one regret. I should have done four reps at 800, I felt like I had two left in the tank, but I stopped at two."

Now that's being "all in."

Being all-in isn't just about time and effort, it's very much about money and being ready to invest in your business.

When I opened my business, I did it in a way that was more classical; I learned this from my dad. I went to Starbucks and spent the day writing my business plan; getting all my ideas down. On paper, I knew exactly how I was going to run the business, the members needed to sustain, the financial plan, everything. At that moment, I was in what you would call "flow state," and within a few hours had written the entire plan out. I had done so much research on opening this business and had all the numbers. Next, I set up an appointment with the Vice President at my local bank. Again, I had never had a business in my life, I was 27 years old, so I needed to follow all the rules. I put on my suit and tie like my dad told me, my wife was there to support me, and my business plan was neatly printed and in my lap. I was ready. The scheduled 15-minute meeting with the Vice President lasted for two and a half hours. I walked away with a $99,500 loan to start the business. Success!

I was so proud that they took a risk on me. An unemployed, never-owned-a-business before, construction manager. Although it seemed like it was a lot of money, I still had to sacrifice much of my own. I topped off my credit cards, wiped my savings out, borrowed from my parents and my wife's parents and threw myself all-in financially too. My gym is located in Scottsdale, Arizona, and if you know this area, you know the rent isn't cheap here. We initially rented a 3,000 square-foot space, and we were paying about $10,000 a month just to have that location. When I opened, I had exactly zero clients, not an ideal situation.

Basically, opening the gym wiped me out. Without my wife working, we would have had to close. She was amazing, and I have to give her praise. She never questioned it, telling me, "Yes, let's do it - let's keep going." We felt that we had this small window of opportunity. I was either going to get another job in construction, or I just run through the window of opportunity to opening the business. This was probably the only chance that we could do this, and we went all-in. We were living on brown rice, eggs and cans of tuna. I know you hear that story all the time, but at the time you're not even thinking of it. I wasn't looking at the rice, eggs, and tuna as if I was too good to eat it every night. It just didn't matter because I couldn't wait to get to work the next day.

I've met many gym owners who seem to be hobbyists. They like working out, and they think they can run a business. But, when things get tough, they don't want to work, they're on vacation, or they're not all-in and that's why they fail. Unfortunately, there are many gym owners whose businesses are on their last breath. We've put together some amazing marketing campaigns for them. In fact, we generated so many leads, they would tell me to shut off the campaigns because they just couldn't get to all the leads we were producing for them. If your business is struggling, you don't want to turn leads away, I'm sorry, but that shouldn't even cross your mind. I even had one gym owner told me that they were on vacation and couldn't get to the leads generated by our marketing program, and demanded we end it early.

Now, it's OK to enjoy your life - don't get me wrong. But not when your business is failing. You need to be all-in. The trend today is to not be all-in, and I'd like to see that change. I want people to focus on what it takes to develop your business. Your business is your baby. Would you take a vacation if your baby was sick and needed you? Neither would I.

During my calls with potential clients, I always ask a lot of questions. Are you all-in? Is this the right time for you to invest in marketing for your current business? Are you truly ready to do it? Is this a do-or-die moment for your business? What are your expectations if you put money and time into marketing your business? Do you understand the time it will take to sign up clients and generate revenue from memberships?

I have yet to meet with a gym owner who says "no" to any of the above questions. They all say, "yes" because they all need the help, otherwise they wouldn't be meeting with me. But sometimes they just aren't ready. We work with clients who are about to lose their businesses and want us to save them. The thing is, a single marketing campaign isn't going to save your business. It's just not. If your business is bad on several levels, and your foundation is crumbling, putting more clients in sometimes accelerates that process, and can make things even worse.

When I work with struggling gym owners, who ARE truly all-in, we can easily turn things around. Some clients we've worked with have told us their success stories of opening their second or third location after we've gotten them back up and running. Some have had to hire several new employees and blow out walls so they can expand their current location. When that foundation is strong, with good marketing, and a business owner who is willing to work hard, we see these businesses thrive.

The one question I ask that tells me a gym owner really knows their business is: "Do you know what your Client Lifetime Value is?" That tells me everything I need to know, and also tells me if I can help that person. Most gym owners don't spend the time to figure out their numbers, and one of the most important numbers when starting out a marketing campaign is Client Lifetime Value. If you know your Client Lifetime Value is $6,000, for example, would you "buy" (spend the money to acquire) that client for $1,000? If they say, "absolutely," then I know what the next question is. "Would you buy that client for $2,000?" And, they start to think about it for a little bit, and think, "Well, if it's worth $6,000 to have that client, sure I'll pay $2,000." You can guess the next question, "Would you be willing to spend $3,000 for that client?" Well, now they start to hesitate. But, I explain, "Well, you're still getting a $3,000 return on your investment." The analogy I use all the time is this: If someone came up to you on the street, with a bar of gold worth $6,000 would you pay $3,000 for it? The answer is always, "yes."

You need to look at your clients as assets to your business; they all have value worth investing in. Not just your time and energy, but your money. If you know what your Client Lifetime Value is, you'll know how much you should be willing to spend. My rule of thumb here is that you should be willing to spend three months of revenue from that client, in order to "buy" that client out of the marketplace. For example, if a client spends $200 a month to train with you, and they're with you for 12 months, they're worth $2,400, so you should be willing to spend $600 on them. That number includes marketing expenses and anything else that goes into making that sale, for example special promotions, or incentives like heart-rate monitors or supplements. In that case, at month four, you're already at a profit.

If I can give just one piece of advice to the future business owner, it's to not open it up as a hobby. You can have a great lifestyle as a gym owner. You're helping other people change their lives. You're helping people solve their health problems. You're helping them slow down and even reverse diseases. You're helping people get off of medication. So, what we do is noble. We're helping save lives. But, if you're not all-in, I recommend doing something else. This business isn't easy, there are a lot of moving parts, and a lot of people look for the magic bullet when it comes to marketing and getting people in the door. It doesn't work that way. You just have to take it seriously. You can't be half-in, you need to be ALL-IN.

Client Lifetime Value Formula (simple):

[Average revenue of each client per month] x [Average number of months a client stays with you] = Client Lifetime Value

Exercise

Do you consider yourself all-in? If so, how?

_____

_____

_____

_____

Do you know what your Client Lifetime Value is, what is it?

_____

_____

_____

_____

What is your current monthly marketing budget?

_____

_____

_____

_____

How much are you willing to spend to acquire a client?

_____

_____

_____

_____

"Whatever is worth doing is worth doing well."

Philip Stanhope, 4th Earl of Chesterfield

Chapter 3

You Need to Market

At first, marketing was not my strength. But I knew it was the absolute key to moving myself into that Business Owner quadrant. Running a business, and leading a great team, and working with clients came naturally to me. It was in built into my DNA. But, learning to market myself and my business was new territory. I had to start from zero, again, so that I could build things into systems and get out of the day-to-day functions as a gym owner.

In the beginning, I hated sales. I hated having to sit in front of somebody and sell something or sell "me" and the brand I was trying to develop. Trying to make that exchange of getting money from a potential client was difficult for me, as it's just not part of my core personality. But I had to learn it, and because I learned it, I learned to love it. Now, I love sales. In fact, one of my favorite things to do now is to sell; to find someone's pain points and give them a solution for that.

There are some basics steps you can take for marketing your business, and your own business timeline will be different from other businesses. But the steps are virtually the same. A key to success is having a Marketing Plan. Just having a pretty sign on your building and being located on a nice road is not a "plan" and it does not guarantee you anything. You really have to have a specific plan to drive leads, and to funnel potential clients through your marketing system. Allow me to dig into this a little bit. Let's say you are offering a paid trial to your gym (something I highly recommend), and you put out marketing to a cold market; people who have never heard of you, and don't know you. From experience, using a paid trial inside of a digital sales funnel with e-commerce built into it, shows me that 3-5% of that target audience will opt-in to receiving information from you. From that group, 25% of that 3-5% will sign-up and pay for the trial online. Once they are in your gym, you should convert 80% of those individuals into an annual member and recurring revenue.

Using that example of conversion percentages, and if you have a specific goal of 10 clients per month from that single strategy, let's look at an example of how you would get there. If your goal is 10 annual members, we need to start backwards to see how this would work. Let's say 1,000 people hit the landing page for the offer, at a 3-5% conversion, 30-50 will opt-in (and become leads), and from there, at a 25% purchase conversion online, 12 people will sign-up for the trial. Once these clients are in your gym, it's now your job to convert 80% of them into members; that's 10 annual memberships. Let's say it costs you $3 per click to get someone on that landing page. That's now $3,000 for Facebook ads to get the initial trial purchased. If you are charging somewhere around $100 for the trial, you will have generated $1200 on the front end. On the surface it's a loss. However, if you can convert 80% of those trial memberships into an annual membership, then you've more than covered your expenses, and now you are adding net revenue.

I know these numbers because I have run more than 6,000 campaigns over the past three years for our marketing clients. The price per click changes, and right now it's on the rise, but it may level out again. If you know the conversion rate of running a marketing promotion, you can safely predict what you will get out of marketing dollars that you spend. If it feels like a loss at the initial trial membership, trust in the 80% conversion into annual client. If you're doing your job right, you stand to make a healthy profit on each campaign you run. In our case those conversions add up to $250 per member, per month.

In the above example of 10 new clients, you're looking at $2,500 each month, around $30,000 gross revenue per year from a single $3,000 ad spend. Within 1-2 months, my initial cost has been covered, and we have added to our gym membership. We also work hard at retaining at least 95-97% of our members every month by building a community at the gym, that initial revenue can grow much higher over time.

If you are running a gym, then you need to have a variety of ways to get people in your gym in the first place. We call this process, "having multiple poles in the water," like on a fishing boat, where you have five or six lines in the water. When done right, one of them strikes or many if you're going through a school of fish. The same thing goes with marketing and growing your business.

A lot of times we're all very naive when we open a business. We think that if people can see us, they're just naturally going to come in the doors, or we hope they visit the website to find out more. Hoping isn't a plan. Number one...people don't know what you do. Number two...they don't know how much you cost. Nobody has experienced your business, yet. There's no customer base, or real social media or community presence at all. You need a way to get them in the door, and we recommend having five or six things working for you, at any given time; five or six poles in the water.

Best-case scenario, all those poles bite. You're eating good that night! But, a lot of times, you have to shift things around. Take social media, for example. Maybe the campaign that was working last month isn't working anymore. Well, you better have something else to pick up the slack.

Let's take a look at some of the things you could be doing to "catch" your clients:

1. Blog content

2. Quality website

3. Joint ventures with local businesses

4. Challenges or Short-Term Specialty Programs

5. Social media marketing campaigns

6. Active social media presence; boost or promote quality content, and direct people to landing page, to 'opt-in'

7. Offer Trial Memberships

8. Client Testimonials/Social Proof

9. Online Reviews. Be proactive with your reviews; ask clients for reviews

10. Visible, big sign out on street front

11. Flyers in nearby neighbourhoods (This is the first thing I did - equipped with door hangers, my camelback, and good shoes, I put door hangers on every door in the neighbourhood. It was pouring rain, during a Monsoon storm and my wife and I would jump out of the truck, knockout 20 houses, jump back in the truck...repeat)

Where do you start? I suggest trying all of them. As long as there's a return on investment, then it makes sense to do it. When my wife and I were hanging all of those flyers on neighbourhood doors, we didn't get 100 clients, but we got a few, and that was worth the effort, because each client was worth a few thousand dollars, AND they may very well bring in other clients at a net cost of zero for us. Bottom line is that you need to get your message out into the market and not just sit back and hope people come to you. Hope is not a strategy. You have to be proactive in your marketing efforts; you have to be aggressive.

In today's world of social media, you really do need to have a strong presence, with high quality content that you give away to potential clients. You should have a prevalent Facebook and Instagram presence, and a YouTube channel if you can. For Instagram and Facebook, post daily, and if you can, hire someone who is in your gym to do it. I don't think it's a good idea to outsource posting content on your behalf to someone who is not working in your business. Your posts need to capture your culture of the day-to-day environment, and an outside agency won't be able to do that for you. Something to remember is not every post should be a sales post; you should be giving away value as often as possible Typically, we balance the content and sales posts 5 to 1; five content posts to one sales pitch. A way to leverage the content you create is to use it across all channels. You can   re-purpose it to be a blog post, a video, an email, and infographic and a Facebook post all from the same piece of content. We lead with content, versus a sales pitch as much as possible. If you have trouble creating content, just listen to what your clients are asking you. Our content often comes from our clients asking questions, and our trainers researching the answers. Then, we can share it and produce high quality content that drives additional business to the gym via the trial-offer. We find that this "leading with content" strategy generally brings in a much higher quality client. I suggest you start listening to your clients, and start creating content as soon as possible.

Having several strategies working for you is the goal. If you rely on only one of the ideas above, you are severely limiting your potential for growing your customer base. Right now, for example, in my marketing and coaching businesses (ProFit Marketing

Solutions) we're tackling several strategies concurrently. First - this book. Written as a guide, and as an introduction on how we built our business. This book will also act as a marketing tool for lead generation, client loyalty and social media marketing. In addition, we have email marketing, additional social media marketing, text message marketing, Facebook Live, speaking engagements, and more. There is not one solution, one magic bullet that will generate all your business. It's time to diversify.

Every week we're taking calls from gym owners who need help growing their membership. They're panicking now because they might have been getting 50-60 clients the same month last year, but this year only two. I ask them what else they have going on as far as marketing, and it's usually nothing. Usually the only tool they have in the works is Facebook advertising, and while I would say that Facebook advertising was probably how most gyms have gotten clients over the last two years, it's changing by the minute, and you need to be ready. A few years ago, you could "limp" into social media, and make a ton of money with Facebook ads. Not today, you can't do it like that anymore. You better have more "poles in the water."

The challenge today is that Facebook advertising is so prevalent that you're not only competing with local gyms, you're also competing with jewelers and car dealerships, restaurants and other companies, for your demographic and potential client's attention. Because of this, you might have to spend 6 times the cost per thousand impressions (CPM) than you would have just a few years ago. That trend is not slowing down anytime soon. The cost will go up and your results will lessen, unless Facebook and Instagram open up additional placements. I don't foresee this happening and I expect the cost will continue to rise. When that happens, you have to have other strategies to fall back on, like the few I've outlined above.

It saddens me to see gym owners suffer so much when their Facebook ads stop working. Gym owners just don't have the time to figure it all out and stay up-to-date with all the changes that happen in the marketing world. There are tools and programs out there to help, including ours. We created the ProFit GPS (Growth. Plan. Strategy.) System, www.profitgps.net, an all-in-one marketing solution. We designed it to help gym owners successfully market their businesses. ProFit GPS is a portal currently housing over 50 different marketing strategies ready to use, complete with Facebook and email content, including recipes, exercises, health tips, funnels and more. The gym owner just has to cut-and-paste. The GPS program also includes complete digital marketing campaigns for low/front end offers, complete with funnels, ads, and email/SMS content to get new clients in the door. It also has client retention strategies, Facebook Messenger Bot marketing that's scheduled and automated, and flash marketing. There are over 50 strategies, and more than half of them do not rely on Facebook or social media traffic. GPS is a solution for marketing from a variety of sources and keeping multiple poles in the water.

A few years ago, I had the thought in relation to our own marketing strategy, "What if Facebook disappeared overnight?" How many businesses would still be able to sustain if Facebook and Instagram went away, if Mark Zuckerberg woke up one morning and said, "You know, I've made enough money, let's just shut this down." As unlikely as this seems, nothing is more consistent in our world than change. I wanted to find a way for us, as a gym, to make sure we could adapt our marketing plan to any major change, or in case our Facebook strategies just stopped working, I went back and looked at everything we had used to gain and keep clientele in the gym. I went back through the past decade of successful marketing campaigns and strategies that got us to where we are and compiled everything. Through that process, we put all those things into one place, with a marketing plan calendar, that laid out the entire marketing process for the whole year. From this, we created a program that helped us not to be so reliant on one strategy working at one time. ProFit GPS was born.

The reason I created this program is because trying to juggle five to six strategies and run a gym, can be a little overwhelming. The bottom line is that you have to constantly generate leads, retain your customers, and do so in a variety of ways. Any tools that you find to help you do this can be well worth your investment. If your gym is just getting started, or if you have an established gym that is struggling, you need to find the tools that have already done the work for you.

In 2009, when I was building our business, we didn't have social media, but somehow, we built up our business. How did we do it? Well, we did it through email marketing, networking, flyers, and other "old-school" marketing techniques. But, when Facebook and other social media marketing platforms came along, we felt like we didn't need to do that hard work anymore. We just needed to pop up a Facebook ad, and "they would come." It wasn't a terrible thing to do, because in the beginning, the return on investment was so high. It's normalizing now, and the return on investment isn't as high as it used to be. Gym owners, who have only been in business for a few years, know no other way to market outside of social media, and that can be a problem.

Let's get back to the basics. One of the basics that can often be overlooked is your gym's culture, and creating a supportive, self-sustaining gym community. Being so enamored with Facebook ads that bring in new client after new client, you can sometimes forget about the current clients that you already have. It really doesn't move your business forward when you're bringing in 10 new clients, but 10 are leaving. You never really grow. We've gotten back to the foundations of what got us here and continue to build on that and diversify our marketing, as well as our client retention efforts. We're having one of our best years, ever.

As you generate leads through your back-to-basics marketing efforts, make sure you have a system to handle them! You can bring in all the leads you want, but if you don't have a system to convert leads to sales, your efforts will be wasted. Additionally, you also have to then be able to handle the load of your new client base. This isn't exclusive to the gym business, it is just basic business sense. If you gain new customers, because of your marketing efforts, you have to be ready for them from the first day they sign-on. Otherwise, all your efforts could crumble if that foundation of business readiness is not there.

This has happened with my business. Early on in my business, we did marketing campaigns where we generated 100's of leads and things just fell apart because we didn't know what to do with all the leads. This exposed the weaknesses in our business, so it was a lesson for us. Marketing exposes whether or not the business foundation is truly sound, or not.

Marketing isn't just a time commitment. As I've mentioned earlier, you also have to commit financially to the process. You should approach marketing as an investment. Something you should go all-in on as well. As a general rule of thumb, count on spending at least 20% of your gross revenue on marketing efforts, every month.

Typically, when businesses start to struggle, marketing is the first thing people cut out of their budget. Which is crazy, and completely backward. If there is one thing that you can put $1 in, and get $2 out, it's marketing. Why wouldn't you invest in marketing? When you are seeing a return, put as much into it as you can. Don't look at marketing as an expense, it's one of the only things you can do to get a return on your investment in your business immediately. Like any investment, it can be a gamble, but if you're doing it right, you are more likely than not to get that money back, and then some. Go all-in!

Exercise

Of the marketing ideas outlined in this chapter, how many are you currently doing?

_____

_____

_____

_____

Which of the marketing ideas will you add to your routine within the next month?

_____

_____

_____

_____

_____

_____

_____

What percentage of your monthly gross revenue is dedicated to marketing? If it's less than 20%, how will you increase your marketing budget?

_____

_____

_____

_____

Update your current marketing plan to include some of the ideas from this chapter. Include monthly and quarterly activities, budgets, and how you'll get it done. Use a separate sheet of paper, or spreadsheet.

"Marketing's job is never done. It's about perpetual motion. We must continue to innovate every day."

Beth Comstock, Vice Chair of GE

Chapter 4

Don't Fall in Love With Your Service

The worst decision I ever made, resulted in the best decision I ever made for my business.

When I first started my business, my dad was by my side when we went to the 2007 IHRSA convention (The International Health, Racquet and Sportsclub Association) in San Diego. You can kind of tell by the name, that this group has been around for a long time, and this is one of the main organizations in the fitness industry. Their annual convention is one of the biggest events in fitness.

In my head, I knew, what kind of fitness business I wanted to have, and I had visited a couple of gym consultants at the convention and hired one. My dad was a consultant, so I had been raised with the notion of "buying" the expertise I did not have from someone who did. To me, this just seemed to be a logical step, and most of the time it is. I did not have any contacts in the industry, so I picked one of the consultants I met at the convention. I thought this consultant was going to be the guy who was going to help me achieve this dream of starting my own fitness business.

Shortly after the convention, he flew out to Arizona and we started looking at different locations. We ran numbers and looked at business models I wanted to pursue. We reviewed spreadsheet after spreadsheet, all the marketing data, everything to visualize what this perfect business was going to look like and feel like. We narrowed it down to two different locations and had plans rendered for both to consider.

Eventually, I selected our location, and got the business up and running. I must have been a genius because the consultant agreed with all my ideas for the new business including location, size, business model, marketing plans, floor plans, equipment layout and projections; something wasn't right, I just didn't know it yet. I felt like I knew front and back, upside down and right side up, that this gym was going to make "x" amount of revenue per month, and I knew exactly what was going to happen. This was in 2009, and we started the business with a specific model that we felt would work. I knew within four months that the business was going to fail. In short, I realized that I had hired the wrong consultant. I almost panicked. I had purchased all new equipment, everything in the place was brand new, so everything I had financially was invested and tied up. I would look at the numbers every week, and just saw a negative death spiral. I knew that I needed to get some help right away or I was going to lose it all. It turns out the consultant I hired was more of a "yes man" than the type of guy I needed.

Fortunately, I had just read a book written by Thomas Plummer, another consultant in the health and fitness industry, and he was speaking close by, in Phoenix, in a few days. I decided to go hear Thomas speak. After his presentation I introduced myself, told Thomas about my gym, and asked if he was taking new clients and how expensive it would be to work with him. Thomas made it easy. He said to gather up my business plan, my "numbers," copies of my marketing material, and layout of the gym and send it to him. He would review the material and said "If I think I can help you, I will set up a one-hour call to discuss it. If we think we can work together, we will go from there."

My first call with Thomas was enlightening. Without malice, he dissected my business model and the things I had done to supplement the dribbling income stream, like "renting" my gym to independent trainers who brought their clients to train on my equipment, in my floor space. He made sure I understood that the independent trainers were taking none of the risk and making all the money. Money that I should be earning for all the risk I was taking.

Over the next few weeks, he helped me understand that the original business model I thought would be so successful would be perfect; but not in the location I had chosen. He noted that, in the business model, I had tried to incorporate a "24-hour come in and train yourself" gym that would sense in a working-class location. But it was not the best model for the neighborhood I had selected, an area that is best described as a high-end, affluent community. Clients in that community would expect more personalized treatment. They would be looking for personal training or small group training where they were known and addressed individually. And, they would be willing to pay for it. Thomas recommended completely changing the gym model to be a personal training studio. Now, I needed someone to show me how to do it.

At this time, Thomas introduced me to Rick Mayo, from Atlanta. I flew out to see Rick and realized quickly he was the right guy to help me make the change. He had opened his doors in 1996, and this was in 2009, so he had already been around the block a few times. Rick had a great model. His gym was about 2,000 square feet bigger than mine, and after 13 years in business, he was raking in over a million per year. I wanted to know what he was doing that I wasn't, and I knew his time was valuable, but I had to save my business. So, I gladly put out the money to spend two days with him.

I shadowed Rick for those two days. He showed me his business, inside and out. He showed me how he trained clients, and literally showed me anything I wanted to know. We went to dinner, and he asked me to sketch out my gym; the layout, the brand-new equipment, every detail I could think of. I asked him, "Well, what would you do with this 3000 square foot space and the fixed equipment in it?" He looked at me and picked up a red marker. One at a time, he started drawing lines through equipment, "Get rid of this…. get rid of this…. get rid of that…."

By the time he was done, I was left with about three pieces of equipment. Again, this was brand new, four-month-old equipment. I must have looked at him as if I was a deer in the headlights, and he said to me, "Space is the best piece of equipment you can have." Of course, Rick was right. If I was to set up my gym to be a personal training gym instead of a self-service type of gym, I needed to make these changes. Rick made it known that in a training gym, you train clients on their feet, and you need to move in multiple directions. "You need all this out of here…. all of it," he repeated.

I owed three years of payments on this equipment. But, again, I knew that my business was failing, so I bit the bullet and liquidated all the equipment that Rick told me to get rid of. I changed the model of the business to one I thought could succeed and never looked back. We instantly lost half of our existing clients because they were coming into the gym to use the equipment. We were basically starting over with the new model. But this was the start of the great success that we have achieved today. A gym that runs itself and has expanded its space to more than double the original size and tripled the revenue.

I can tell you that if I was so in love with my original business, if I had been married to that original plan that I spent almost two years creating, I would not be in business today. It wasn't working. I would have definitely failed and may very well have lost everything. So, when you start your business, or you look at where your established business is right now, and something is not working, there's a reason for it. Something has to change, and it may need to be a dramatic change.

On the surface, this kind of goes against my "work hard and your efforts will be rewarded" philosophy. I was working hard, and we did have a lot of clients, so my hard work was paying off. But the original model was $29-$39/month membership, and now our average client pays $275/month. So, our client numbers were going up at the beginning, but it wasn't sustainable; paying off the expensive equipment that wasn't working for us and added to the fiscal disaster to come.

When we changed the model to a personal training model, we increased our pricing, and had $200-$400 programs, so every client was worth more to me because they were paying 10 times as much as the original model. That increase in revenue, with initially fewer clients, is what allowed us to grow, and help more people.

If I had been stubborn and so in love with my product when meeting Rick, I would have said, "Hell no, man. I'm not getting rid of that. That's all super-expensive equipment." But I needed to do it. In your case, it might be unnecessary equipment. It might be your logo. It might be your website. It might be your business model. It could be anything that you are "married" to but is no longer serving you. It's taking business away from you, revenue and profits. It's taking your future away from you.

Don't be so in love with your business that you're not willing to take a hard look at what's really working or not. These are just business decisions. You have to keep your emotions out of decisions that will determine your fate; you must put your ego aside. Instead of being in love with your business, be in love with positive results. Be willing to tear down what's not working and rebuild things into a business that will work for you. If you choose to live in the past, you could easily find yourself failing.

There are many well-known examples of this. Formerly successful companies that failed to evolve. Compaq Computer, Sports Authority, Blockbuster

Video, Toys-R-Us, BlackBerry, Sears and Roebuck. They might still be in the mix, but some former powerhouses are mere bit players now. Many are gone.

Making these changes was not easy. It was a gut-wrenching time for us when we made the business model change that we did. I remember trying to figure out how to communicate the reasons we were making the changes that we did. We held a seminar at the gym. We sent a letter to everyone, as well as an email, along with signs in the gym. Our goal was to highlight that these changes were being made to benefit our clients. Let's be honest, if clients that have been failing with their fitness in the past, just go to the gym, and play around on the equipment by themselves, without guidance, they're not really going to get the results that we could get them. We were changing our model to be less equipment-based, and more service-based. More results based, and we communicated it this way.

To help ease the transition for our clients, we included a free month so that they could try out the new model. We lost 75% of our clients because they were looking for the original model; a cheap gym where they could do their workouts. When we started, we wanted everyone as a client. We thought we wanted to train everyone. What we learned, thankfully quickly enough, was that we only wanted a certain type of client.

I remember when I was removing equipment and was eyeing the leg press machine. Now, here's a huge piece of equipment where we could train three people in that space. A gym member said to me, "You get rid of that leg press, and I'm canceling my membership." And he did. Sometimes I would be faced with an angry client, and I understood. Most of us don't like change, and they were used to something different. That massive change was the best decision I made for my business and for those clients that left. We weren't really a good fit for them, anyway.

Now, we had the space, most of the remaining members upgraded to a higher rate of service, so a more expensive monthly membership, and we could grow and invest in the company. Some of these clients have become lifetime members. We still have clients today who stayed with us through that transition and we most likely wouldn't have been able to keep them this long without changing the model like we did.

There's a difference between being in love with your business, and loving aspects of your business. There's nothing wrong with that. For example, I love the clients that are with us now. They are amazing. They come in, they're happy, they love being here. The coaching team is wonderful. In fact, the business is not an anchor on me, it's self-sustaining and thrives on the systems we've put into place. If the team needs me, I'm in the office, but I don't need to be "pressing the buttons" anymore. I love being free to keep my own schedule. I bet that if I went on vacation for three months, the business would grow, because now, I'm usually the one who gets in the way. I had finally moved into the Business Owner quadrant.

Exercise

What is it that you love about your business?

_____

_____

_____

_____

_____

_____

_____

What's not working? Why?

_____

_____

_____

_____

_____

_____

_____

What changes do you need to make in your business, NOW, to make it more successful?

_____

_____

_____

_____

_____

_____

_____

What challenges will your business face if you make those changes?

_____

_____

_____

_____

_____

_____

_____

Do you think your business can truly thrive if you
DON'T make those changes?

_____

_____

_____

_____

_____

Is your business going to help you achieve your place
in the cashflow quadrant?

_____

_____

_____

_____

_____

"Don't be afraid to give up the good to go for the great."

John D. Rockefeller

Chapter 5

Get Out of the Way

When I talk about the cashflow quadrants, and I am asked how long it takes to get from "Self-Employed" to "Business Owner," I sometimes have to give the hard answers. Honestly, some people will never get there. They're so hung up on the technical or technician side of their business, they are so hands-on, and because they have that mentality, they just won't get out of their own way. They can't delegate and create a team to service the clients, so they just never get there.

There are plenty of people who run their own training for clients until they are in their 50s and 60s, and then they retire. Unfortunately, that means they

never had their own business that could generate passive income for them, they never became a Business Owner.

Sometimes, gym owners try to build a busines where they can be hands-off but just can't do it. Maybe they don't know how, or they don't like working that way and go back to training again, because that's what they truly love. If that's what you want, then that's totally ok, nothing wrong with that.

I think that if a gym owner wants to get from the "Self-Employed" quadrant to the "Business Owner" quadrant, and they are extremely focused, they can get there quickly. It takes getting all the pieces in place, knowing how to sell, having a great foundation and a having a great team, and developing the systems. Then it can be done. It just takes getting out of your own way and letting go of some control.

It took me six years to do this; through trial and error, mostly. But, knowing what I know now, if a gym owner has that desire, I can help.

Take a look at what you do every day. Take out a sheet of paper and keep it with you for two straight days. Write out everything you do on a daily basis. Do you answer the phones, perform outreach for your clients, do the sales, create Facebook campaigns, train clients, run to the store for supplies, design programs? Write out everything. Once you have everything written out for two days, take a look at all the tasks and start making some decisions. You need to look at what tasks that you absolutely must

do. Do they make you money directly or can someone else do those tasks? If there are items you can delegate, you need to do that immediately. If you don't have an Admin on your team, that would be someone you should look to hire and bring in. Even if it's a part time role for now, and you should delegate the non-income producing tasks to the Admin. This will allow you to free up time for you to focus on generating revenue for your business. Once you have the time, you can start to create systems on how the business should operate without you involved. You don't need to do every little task in your business. If you want to get out of the Self-Employed quadrant, this is your first step. Get out of your own way.

Exercise

List your current team and their primary duties.
Include yourself.

_____

_____

_____

_____

_____

_____

_____

What tasks are you doing now, in your business, that
a team member could do?

_____

_____

_____

_____

_____

_____

Do you need to consider hiring team members, or outsourcing certain tasks to off-site vendors? If so, which tasks?

_____

_____

_____

_____

_____

_____

"You've gotta find a way to get out of your own way, so you can progress in life."

Steve Carlton

Chapter 6

Surround Yourself with the Like-Minded

I surround myself with successful gym owners. That includes Mastermind groups, and people like Rick Mayo - my original mentor, who showed me how to fundamentally change my gym. Rick also runs the Mastermind group that I'm in. There are about 30 of us in that group, and I know that if I ever have a question or something doesn't feel right about an aspect of the business, that I can ask the group and get 15-20 responses within an hour. The members of the Mastermind tell me what they would do if they were in the same position, or maybe something similar that happened with them. There is a genuine camaraderie, that is priceless. One of the best things I've done as a business owner is to join a group like this.

Over the years, I've found that the times I grew the most were when I surrounded or aligned myself with people who were more successful than me. That's usually the key. If you're the most successful person in a group, you need to go to another group. Things come up that I haven't faced before, even after ten years in this business, and one of the best things I've invested in is being part of mentoring groups to help me navigate through issues that may come up. My personal experience is that everybody in these types of groups truly cares about your success, and is more than happy to give helpful advice, share stories and ideas.

Without a group like this, you're on your own to figure things out. Unless you're part of a franchise, which is technically a type of Mastermind group, you're really swimming, alone, with the sharks. You can easily make a bad decision, and not even be aware of it until it's too late. Why not talk with people who are trying to achieve the same things you are and who may have made the same mistakes you're about to? Having a supportive network of business owners, who are shooting for similar goals, in the same field, can help you to avoid your own pitfalls, and you can help other business owners on their way.

Even if you don't join a formal Mastermind group, I think it's critical to network with business owners and people who are like-minded. There are 10 times more ideas and experiences in a group of ten than just what you have under your belt. These are the people who will help you drive your business forward, because you will get stuck, eventually. You might run into an employee, or client issue, that you're just not sure how to deal with. There might be legalities that you haven't considered. Maybe there is someone in your network who has dealt with something similar. Why trek out there alone? Instead of making a split decision, tap into a support system. When I do that, I usually do things right, and make good decisions.

Don't think these groups just take an occasional visit with each other. There must be constant interaction, opportunities to ask questions, get answers, and give answers, on an almost daily basis. No doubt, this will take some of your time, but think of it as your own 15, 20, 30 or more private consultants, who KNOW what you're going through.

I also recommend going outside of your industry, for masterminds. For example, I tune into several podcasts, one of my favorites being MFCEO, with Andy Frisella. I'll listen while I'm driving to work or working out at the gym. Andy speaks my language about things like; work-ethic, how your feelings sometimes just don't matter, winning the day, business drive, and other things that I believe in. He's not offering me anything new, these are things that I think about already. But now, I have someone telling me this in a different way, sometimes in a way that motivates me more deeply, and helps me stay on track. I need a kick in the ass, sometimes, like anybody else. I do sometimes laugh, though. What's happened to me? I used to work out to heavy metal bands like Pantera and Metallica, but now I'm listening to business podcasts. Life sure has changed.

Another group I joined was a business owner group called, Inner Circle, that met in Boise, Idaho, four times a year. We represented all sorts of industries and business models, and we focused mainly on digital marketing. All the businesses were very successful. The investment to be in that group was not inexpensive, I think around $25,000/year. But I will tell you, I made back that investment, twice, in the first meeting. My mentor in that group was a man named Russell Brunson, and he taught me how to run the Perfect Webinar, and I made $50,000 in two weeks.

Russell gave an opportunity, to fewer than 100 motivated business owners, to participate in group meetings facilitated by him. Part of each meeting was given to individual owners to present their business to the group and talk about what areas needed help, or what area was recently highly successful. Russell would take lead in offering suggestions for potential changes or enhancements that could be beneficial. His observations, based on years of experience and the wisdom gained by reviewing and helping hundreds of individual businesses, was worth every bit of the cost of participation. But, as an added bonus, all the other owners could also offer suggestions, and some of their input was every bit as valuable. If given an opportunity such as this one, consider it for you and your business.

When you're an entrepreneur, you're on a figurative island. A lot of times, you're on your own. There's nobody watching you to make sure you're doing what you're supposed to be doing. It can be a lonely place. If you're not self-motivated, then being an entrepreneur is the wrong thing to do. Because, guess what? When things get "hard," and you need to take a little break, the next thing you know, nobody's holding you accountable, and something fails.

That's where Masterminds come in. That's where networking comes in. That's where Mentors and Coaches come in. We all like to think we're internally motivated, but all of us need external motivation as well, some of us more than others. So, I recommend hiring a mentor or coach like myself. If you're connecting with the right people you ALWAYS get a return on your investment, just like with marketing. At first, in the gym group, I didn't think I needed that kind of support. I felt I needed it more in the digital marketing aspect of the business. But both have been so beneficial and helpful.

I had almost let my ego get in the way when I first joined the Fitness Mastermind group because I was almost already doing seven-figures in my business. Thank goodness I was able to fit my head through the door because I assumed I wouldn't need help from anyone. Fortunately, I opened up and joined the group. There are business owners in that group who have helped me out tremendously.

Being a part of these groups has helped me bring my thinking to another level that would not have been possible, otherwise.

You know, good advice is just good advice; unless you take action on it. Keep your ear to the ground on what's working in your industry, and what's not. Be ready to evolve at any moment. Understand and share your industry's best practices, with people who have been through it, or are going through it with you. If you're a gym owner, you need to be in a gym owner Mastermind group, not a personal trainer Mastermind group, for example. If you're a trainer currently, and are looking to open and own a gym, you need to join the business owner, gym owner group, in my opinion. Find people who are ahead of you, in that case. Don't be the smartest person in the room.

Every time you turn around, there's somebody trying to sell you something. Everybody's a "guru." But, so much of the time, these so-called experts aren't really experts at all. They've never run a successful business outside of their consulting, maybe. These "gurus" have never had employees, had client issues, or worked the day-to-day grind that it takes to build a business. But, yet, they're going to teach you and coach you how to do it, and I don't see this trend slowing.

Be wary of who's trying to sell you something. This hits a nerve with me because some of the best consultants out there, like a Todd Brown, who I talk about in a later chapter, aren't the ones trying to push their ideas down your throat. They're offering practical advice, based on their own success in the business that you're in, or just business wisdom, in general.

There's only one person responsible for who influences you, and that's you. For example, because I'm a gym owner, I'm actually a target demographic for marketers who are offering services trying to help gyms. I get emails, cold-calls, and text messages from people who have never been there. I don't know who they are, and I shake my head. Why would I want to buy their advice when I don't see a successful gym behind their name? I don't see them in the fitness industry creating a successful business. Typically, the "experts" who are trying to teach you stuff, aren't really experts at all.

This is a problem for organizations that are founded on the model of people becoming coaches before they become business owners. And, by becoming a coach first, they then become a business owner, and haven't even built a successful, well-established business. I will have opened the gym more than 10 years ago, by the time this book is released, and I've just about seen it all, lived it all, made my own mistakes, learned from those mistakes, and built a community within and outside of the gym. I always have things to learn, and I'm always open to listening to an influencer. But not if they have never run something or started a business from zero and then built that business into an established organization.

I understand that everyone is trying to make money and make a living, and even that many of these consultants are truly trying to help people. However, if I'm the customer, why would I buy from somebody who has never been there? If I'm trying to get to a specific place, I want to follow someone who's already gotten there, Thomas Plummer for example, as I mentioned above, a "grandfather" to many of today's consultants. A speaker, consultant and coach, and in the very early days, I would have calls with him. Everything that he told me to do, including introducing me to Rick, typically worked. He got me out of the hole, time after time. He also looks at big picture things, like retirement, and your life. So, in a way, he influenced me to ultimately join up with Masterminds.

Let me give you an example of how my Mastermind group has helped me. I had a situation with my Fitness Director. He is basically my right-hand man, and without him, I would be back working in my gym. He was dealing with some medical issues and had to have surgery that his insurance was only going to partially pay. Neither he nor I could afford the rest. Many clients were coming up to me to ask how they could help out. I felt like I was in a weird position; do I ask my clients if they can help my staff with a medical bill situation? I honestly didn't know what to do. Ten years in the business, and I had never seen this situation come up in a book about running a business.

I asked the Mastermind group for their advice. As I was recording the quick video to ask for advice, I was getting answers, and they were brilliant. So, we put together a charity bootcamp where clients, who could help financially, were able to sign-up, and it didn't put anyone who couldn't under any pressure. We raised more than $6,000 for Zach before we even held the event and eventually funded what was needed. The advice also included the tip to have a client, who really championed the idea, basically run the program and event instead of it coming directly from me. The group helped me through a sensitive situation, and in a way, that client won, the staff won, and the gym wins because Zach got the support that he needed to help cover his medical expenses. I, most certainly, couldn't have come up with an idea this good by myself. Something that wasn't clear at all became crystal clear, and the clients loved it. We also solidified the sense of community at our gym, another bonus.

Two brains are better than one and 30-50 are even better!

Exercise

Do some research on local, regional and online business network and support groups. Fill in their information (website, phone number, annual or monthly membership fees):

- Mastermind

_____

_____

_____

_____

_____

- BNI (Business Network International)

_____

_____

_____

_____

_____

- Chamber of Commerce

_____

_____

_____

_____

_____

- Other:

_____

_____

_____

_____

_____

"Mastermind and collaborate with other smart entrepreneurs if they have futures that are even bigger than their present."

Yanik Silver

Chapter 7

Leadership is More Than Being a Boss

Something I learned pretty early in my business is the limitations of my effectiveness. Just because you're the boss, doesn't mean you're a leader. What I mean is, being a leader is more than just making decisions. It's having the team behind you to support your vision. I think this goes back to when I was involved in sports; I was always the captain of every team I was on, and I think it was because I put the work in, and I didn't think I was above anyone else.

Granted, I'm the owner of the gym, I'm the owner of the marketing company, but I'm not above anybody else. Most organizations have either an informal or formal organizational chart. There is a hierarchy in the two businesses that I own, but it doesn't mean that I'm not going to work, side-by-side with my team. First of all, I enjoy it and I love working hard. Plus, I know there's a job to be done, and there's not one job that I ask my team members to do, that I haven't done myself. From taking the trash out, to going to pick up copies at the printer, running Facebook ads for clientele, to making a sales call or doing the books.

Every single thing that is being done in both businesses, I have done at one time. In the beginning of each business, I had to. But, more importantly, I'm not above doing any of the work. So, being a leader means that you're all-in, and you're not above anyone else on your team. It means treating your team as equals. They're all people, they're trying to be financially successful, and trying to live their lives. In fact, in my marketing business, I've structured it in a way that we don't keep time on anyone, we don't "punch the time clock" in order to get paid; if there is a job to get done, we just get it done.

With the marketing company, I run that business in a really unique way. Everybody is on salary, and there are no specific hourly requirements. Staff can take vacation whenever they want, as long as the job gets done. I don't care where staff are, they can be in Hawaii or Australia, as long as they have their computer, stay connected, and are available when we need them. But, bottom line, if the job's done, I don't care what they do. I don't micromanage, and I think more work gets done with this overall hands-off approach. Sometimes the work setting is fairly relaxed, and sometimes we're all working triple-time to get projects launched. But the work gets done - that's all that matters.

The gym is a different story. Because we have specific hours for the gym, and clients have training times, we have to be a bit more structured. But we have some unique structures there, as well. For example, typical gyms assign one coach to one client. At our gym, a client can train with any coach. So, that works out if someone is sick, or if they've gone on vacation, it's just not a problem, and it can benefit the client, as each trainer has specific and unique skill sets. For any absences, the entire team picks up the slack, and everybody's OK with that. This creates a team effort and increases the camaraderie of the team, as a whole.

I believe that it's my job to be a leader, but also to create a culture of leadership where everyone can take on a leadership role. It's important to create this type of community because, the only way a company really grows, is if you have a team of leaders. In order to facilitate this, the best thing you can do, is not get upset with an employee if they make the wrong decision. Instead, get upset if they don't make a decision.

I'm OK if you make the wrong decision, as long as you're going 100-mph, the wrong way. Just go all-in. If that's what you thought was the right thing to do at the time, and you made the decision, I'm never going to get mad if it doesn't work out. Especially, if you committed yourself to the decision and worked hard implementing it.

If you empower your team to make decisions, you'll see how fast your company can grow. And, not every decision is going to be right. In fact, they're never always going to right or perfect. But I support that decision. If I can understand the thought process at the time, even if it's wrong, I'm still supporting the person. We chalk it up as a learning opportunity and move on. It's critical to build a culture where people feel confident in being creative, and that they feel like they can move on their own. If that doesn't exist, you are limiting your company, and your staff. Surrounding yourself with self-starters can only be sustained if they feel that their "starts" and decisions will be supported.

Being a leader is a way of life. Not a task. It's just how you do things in your organization. For example, are you available to your team? Or, do you disappear on them? Are you supporting their decisions? Are you micromanaging? When you're just starting your business, are you there? Physically there? Are you the face of the business?

I have always been that face. I was the one mopping the floor between sessions and putting equipment away. I'd carry in the water from my truck, and clients loved that. They loved seeing that, and they respected, and loved to support that. As you grow, you start to slide away from direct client activity, and more into taking care of the business operations. When that happens, you're going to hear about it, and it may not feel very good.

It hit me hard here. We were getting very successful and I was not needed as much, as my team was running the show. My core group of clients that I had personally trained in the past, when the gym first started, they weren't seeing me around as much. They started to feel that the business had grown too much, and that they were now a "number" versus a person.

There's a line in the sand, and every new client coming in from that point on doesn't even really know who I am - other than a text message welcoming them to the gym when they join. But, the older clients, some of them got upset, and it almost seemed as if they didn't want to see me succeed. They would rather see me mopping the floor than running a team. That's unfortunate, but it's going to happen.

This was something I brought to my Mastermind group, and I received 10 responses almost immediately. I was told that sometimes that happens, people see you succeeding, and, if they aren't in their own lives, they lash out at others. It was reassuring to hear that I shouldn't worry about it, because it's going to happen, and it's inevitable as the gym grows. Once again, we're finding the clients that we really need, and the clients where this isn't going to work for them are going to move on, naturally. It's OK. If you want to grow, you have to be willing to let go of some clients.

I wasn't doing anything wrong, we were doing everything right for the business. The clientele saw me starting the new company and felt like the mom-and-pop business had lost its way. I did lose key clients that I would rather have not lost. Every client is important, especially those that supported me since the beginning. If I had to do it over, my communication with clients would have been better. For those clients who are going to be affected by your success, let them know and have that conversation with them. We're in the business of people, and clients are going to express what they're feeling inside, outward, toward you, and even if it has nothing to do with you. Having those conversations, and understanding the consequences, good or bad, of any decision you make, is part of being a leader in your business.

You may lose key clients. You may even lose good employees. But, your job, as a leader, is to make decisions on what's good for the business. You need to take responsibility for keeping your business going so that your employees and their families feel secure. Your responsibility is to be around in the future for your current clients, and new clients. The whole point is to create a business that continues past your involvement. Only a leader can create that model. Otherwise, you're just an employee of your business.

The fitness business is different than many others out there. For one, it's very personalized. You're seeing the same people every day, and they get to know you. It's not like you're making a widget, putting it in a box, and shipping it out. There's a name and face to your customers; this is about their life, your life. They know everything about you, and there are relationships that are built. I would have thought my clients would be happy about my success, and most were. But, for some, it was just the opposite, and that's tough to deal with. I was literally told once, that a client was leaving because I wasn't mopping the floors anymore.

But, overall, the gym is a community. For most of your clients, the gym, and their time working out, is a big part of their life. You start to understand how important it is to maintain that sense of community. When that happens, not only are your clients attached to the gym, they get attached to the ownership and the training team, and they also get attached to the other clients. This is a great thing to have, because they support each other, inside and outside of the gym. There are numerous friendships that develop because of time spent at the gym. That goes with me, too. I have wonderful friends, who have been in my life for years, that I met "at the gym" somewhere. There have been engagements, marriages, babies, job opportunities, friendships; all stemming from the community that we've made at the gym.

We always say we want to be the "third place." Work, home and gym. We want to be the third place in that person's day. For some people, that third place may be Starbucks, or the local bar, or a movie theatre. There are things you can do to build that community, and be a leader in your own gym community, like having events that have nothing to do with being at the gym. For example, we have an annual Holiday Party where the gym shuts down, we have an open bar, a raffle, casino tables, and a DJ. We sponsor a Toys-for-Tots toy donation drive. We celebrate milestones and goals that our clients reach with pictures and videos in the Hall of Fame. Now that client is really connected, they have their name on the wall and they're wearing a special shirt bragging about their achievement. Now they have buy-in. Why would they go anywhere else? Their name is on the wall! When you build a strong community, you will have a high client retention rate, upwards of 95% or higher, because you're taking care of the people within your gym.

We also have sponsored charity events. There's no better way to lead the community than to help each other out. This can happen at any time of the year when a client is in need. The four-year-old nephew of one of our gym members was facing heart transplant surgery. As a father of a young child, I can't even imagine what that family was going through, having to face the prospect of a heart transplant. Which means another very young child has lost his or her life, as well, and what that family is going through. We wanted to do what we could to help this client, and planned a charity event, and were able to raise $4,000 for the expenses that the family had to cover. Expenses like; parking at the hospital where they were having the procedure done, meals, travel, lodging; anything they needed to get through this hard time.

When people were coming together, locking arms in support of a fellow community member, it was not only heartwarming, it added to everyone's sense of belonging at our gym. Leading and building this type of community and seeing opportunities to build and strengthen your gym community, creates a warm, rewarding environment for everyone. Ownership, staff, clients and their families. If, as a leader, you forget to create this sense of community in your gym, this sincere connection with and between your clients, you'll struggle.

You can have a great location, a fabulous website, a cool logo, and amazing equipment. Without a sense of community, you run the risk of clients leaving you for the next new gym that opens in your town. When you create something special, something that acts as that third place, you've created an environment that is an important part of your clients' lives and there is no substitute for that.

Exercise

What are you currently doing in your gym to create a sense of community with your clients?

_____

_____

_____

_____

_____

_____

Your employees?

_____

_____

_____

_____

_____

_____

What types of activities and/or structures will you implement to add to a sense of community for your employees and clients?

_____

_____

_____

_____

_____

_____

"If everyone is moving forward together, then success takes care of itself."

Henry Ford

Chapter 8

If You Stop Learning, You Stop Growing

Every industry changes. It may mean you have to look at a different marketing medium or strategy or a different service altogether. Maybe it's new products to replace those that are now outdated. I think that more has changed in the last 10 years for the fitness industry than it has in the last 50 years prior to that. What I mean by that is that over the past 10 years, there has been a massive shift in how people train and the equipment used, as well as the business models found in today's environment. If you're still stuck in the "old school" ways, you're going to miss the boat for the NEXT trend.

One of the things that we do at our gym is to always make sure that we are all continuing to learn. We take the whole team to seminars, we'll drive or fly to industry conferences, go to different speakers, do different workouts, and look at the latest and greatest science around fitness. The things that we do today in the gym, we wholeheartedly believe are the best that we can do, based on current knowledge out there, for our clients. Ten years from now, we may look back and think "Man, that was some stupid stuff we were doing back then." But, TODAY, the research supports what we're doing and why.

We know that what we're doing now will change. Ten years from now, if we're doing the same exact thing for our clients as we're doing today, I guarantee you that we've missed the boat, and we will lose clients, business, and revenue. If we're evolving in how we train, based on strong research, and educating our clients about why we're making changes, our client base will appreciate the work and learning that we are doing, on their behalf.

The same goes for marketing. Right now, the trend is social media, it's social advertising and Instagram followers. But I can tell you, within a few years, it may very well be something else, and something completely different. It might be a marketing device we don't even know exists yet. I hear this from marketing clients all the time, "Well, things that were working in 2017 aren't working for me anymore, two years later."

Well, guess what? You better find the next thing. Because, if you don't find it, you're stuck and you're going to waste time, money and you're going to stay still. If you stop learning, you stop growing. That goes for EVERY aspect of your business. You will never be wasting your time or money to stay on top of your industry, and on top of marketing trends.

This isn't just about you, you need to involve your team as well. Your entire team has to be involved. Remember, if you want to truly move from the Self-Employed quadrant to the Business Owner quadrant, you have to empower your team to make decisions. They can't make those decisions, or at least not good decisions, if they are not educated with the latest information out there. We communicate to our employees, from day one, and it's in our employee manual, that they can expect from the leadership to be heard, and that they have decision making powers and responsibilities.

We include the entire team in the decision-making process. So, for example, when the team returns from the event, or workshop or conference, we meet at the gym. Everyone gets an opportunity to share what they learned and felt was important to bring back to the gym. We'll make decisions, together, based on what we learn. Not only does this build the strength of the team, but it also creates this really positive work environment where employees feel heard and see changes that they suggested being implemented in the business.

I think fundamental to the success of your business is letting your team know that they have a voice in the business. I'll be the first to admit that I don't know everything. You'd be the same way, I hope. Each of your team members sees everything through a different lens than you. You have to be willing to step outside of your own box and understand that there are many ways to do the same thing, and some are just better than others. Listen and take action on team members' ideas.

Think of your first job, or second, or even third. Did your boss implement ideas you came up with? Did they solicit your opinion or advice? If they didn't, can you imagine what it would have felt like if they had? So often, employees hear the lie coming from their supervisors, "We care about you, we listen to you, your opinion matters." But the bottom line is that it doesn't. It goes a long, long way to actually set up a business environment where the opposite is true. Team members are valued, appreciated and listened to, and EVERYONE is involved in learning and growing together in the business, and for the business.

Planning for continuing education is a routine part of every year in the business. There are certain seminars and workshops that we attend. Those may change from time to time, as the industry changes. But the bottom line is that every person in the business attends, together, and we meet afterwards, every single one of us, together, to figure out our action plan. We then implement, together, the idea, based on what we all learned and agreed to support.

Another way to support this is to pay for continuing education. If it makes sense for the business, for instance, for somebody to get a nutrition certification, we'll pay for that. That coach has learned something, so their abilities and skills have grown, plus now we've grown the variety of services we can offer. We've done that with; Golf Performance Certification, Stretch Therapy Certifications, Titleist Performance Institute, Precision Nutrition, and FMS Certifications. These certifications aren't cheap. But we'll pay for it because it's that important.

We make sure to protect the business so that we don't educate someone who then promptly leaves and opens their own business or moves to a competitor. We have an educational allowance agreement of terms for the employee to continue working, in the business, for a minimum of six months after the completion of the program or certification. If the employee separates or leaves the business, the educational allowance is paid back. Outlining the terms also helps to set expectations because, if the employee were to leave with that certification, it doesn't help the business anymore.

Just a couple of years into the business, we took the team out to Long Beach, California, for a Perform Better Seminar. Now, this event is split into half lecture, and the other half hands-on workouts. Before we left, everyone got to choose their own activities, while we made sure that the business-minded people were in the business-minded stuff, and the hands-on people were in the hands-on workshops. When we were driving back from that trip, the team was on fire, and we are all so excited. We were talking with clients, "You'd better be ready! We're coming back with some big stuff!"

It melded the team together in such a way that drove our momentum into the fourth quarter, and we ended up having one of our best overall years. This was in our old space, and when we got back from that seminar, the programming changed, some of the equipment changed, the excitement in the gym increased. I was agreeing with all of it. When we met after the seminar, I remember sitting in my chair while we were sharing what we learned and our new ideas. I was thinking, "Dang, we should be doing ALL of this!" And, we knew going in that we were doing great things, but we always ask ourselves, "Can we be better? Can we do better?"

Everyone went in with an open mind, and everyone came out of that seminar with a new commitment to our clients and our business. I bought some new equipment. And, all of this was done together, as a team, learning and growing. And, our business grew and expanded, eventually causing us to more than double our space.

Sometimes I hear someone say, about their job, "Oh, jeez, I HAVE to go to work tomorrow." This thought just never crosses my mind. If I hear someone on our staff say something like this, maybe under their breath, to a friend or on the phone, it hurts, and sometimes I even just want to fire someone like that. But, that's then my fault, and maybe something I need to look at. Am I truly giving that person the opportunity to learn and grow in the business?

But, when your team is super excited to get to work, and they're beating you to work, and loving what they do, then you know you're doing it right. Now, we all know that some days are harder than others, and there are some days where maybe you just don't feel good, or are not up to going to work, but overall it needs to balance out as a business owner, or employee. Overall, you need to love going to work. There's nothing more damaging than a team, or team member, who hasn't bought into your vision. On the other hand, there's nothing more amazing than having a team who is working together, with you, to provide the best possible experience and service (or product) for your clients.

Those team members are bringing up great ideas. They're coming in early. They're staying late. They're helping clients. When you see that, as a business owner, that's about the best feeling you can have, especially when you see it on a day-to-day basis. When you're in business, obviously you want to make money, support your family, support your lifestyle, and make a living. You have to remember that the 10 or 20 people working for you want the same thing. So, you have to create an environment where they feel that they're accelerating and they're making enough money to support themselves.

This may take a complete culture shift in your business. Unfortunately, in the fitness industry, for example, it's a very common thing to have a coach come in, train a bunch of clients, and then have a whole of clients run off with them as they start a new business or go to a competing gym. Even if you have everything ready to go with non-disclosure, confidentiality and non-compete contracts, at some point, someone is going to challenge and test you to find out if you're going to do something about it.

As much as I've usually felt that I'm doing things right, this very scenario happened to me a few times earlier in the business. And, each time, it crushed us. I'm not talking about a couple of clients leaving. I mean that we would have $10,000/month of revenue and client support gone, overnight. I've learned from the mistakes in the early days, and now have created and nurtured a positive culture. The team we have now is the best team we've ever had. We don't have one, or more, bad apples in the bunch that are ruining it for everyone else and spoiling the culture.

If you ever get that bad apple. That person who is NOT learning and growing with you and with your business, and who is complaining to clients, to other coaches, to staff, to anyone who will listen, you just have to nip that in the bud. Quickly. For instance, I had a coach who we followed each other on Instagram. She posted a video about training clients and she was in the video at another gym. I forwarded the video to my Directors and asked them if they knew anything about it. Neither of them knew. The Fitness Director set up a meeting with the three of us; the Coach, the Program Director and me.

It turned out to be something completely unrelated to her work at our gym and wouldn't result in any loss of clientele. In fact, it was online work that we already knew she was doing, and during the meeting, she said, "No way in heck would I ever leave this place." She apologized that it might have looked like that, and it was a clear misunderstanding. But, five years ago, I would have fired that trainer so fast, and I would have been wrong. So, yes, nip things like this quickly, but make sure you're right, and that you're making a good decision for everyone concerned, as well as the business.

The very first coach I ever hired back in 2009, worked closely together with me. I would do the marketing, make the sale, and then send the client over to the her. We were doing great, and I was giving her client, after client, after client. I wasn't watching close enough; she was building personal relationships with all the clients I had given her and telling them that she was going to open her own place.

As you can guess, one day she didn't show up for a 2:00 p.m. appointment, but neither did her client. I don't think much of it, wondering if maybe the schedule was just screwed up. I reached out and called her - no answer. The next hour, same thing happened, and I'm still not getting a return call. What she did was to make deals with every one of the clients, and one day, that day, she switched over to a garage gym, of all places. Every client knew about it, I lost virtually all of my business overnight. There were a few clients who knew it was the wrong thing to do, but the point of my story is that this can very well happen to you if you don't have your business in order.

The way to fight that is to have open communication and have a great culture, a learning and growing culture, with your team. Because, if not, guess what? Everyone will just be looking out for themselves, and they're going to steal your clients. I don't want to paint a horror story, because that's not the point of this book. But it really is something you have to be aware of, and by giving EVERY member of your team the opportunity to contribute, learn and grow, you can avoid a tragedy.

A way to think of this is if your employees feel alone, if they just feel like they're planets revolving around your sun, then they may very well drift off, and you lose a core of your business. On the contrary, if you create a strong, unified culture, anybody who comes into the team and isn't open to being a part of that type of team, they may not stay too long, or they may not even take the job in the first place.

Exercise

How do you demonstrate to your team that you are listening to their ideas?

_____

_____

_____

_____

_____

_____

What is the decision-making process in your business?

_____

_____

_____

_____

_____

_____

How have trends in the fitness industry changed since you first started the business?

_____

_____

_____

_____

_____

When was the last industry conference you attended with your team? What takeaways did you come back with? Have you implemented those ideas?

_____

_____

_____

_____

_____

_____

"It's what you learn after you know it all that counts."

John Wooden

Chapter 9

Use Core Values as Your Compass

A lot of new businesses have gotten away from the "old-school" ways of doing business, and skip over having a mission statement, or core values, or a philosophy. I think this is a really bad idea and you can find yourself and your business "off track" really quickly without them.

Let's talk about core values. These are not the same as your personal values; these are the values that everyone in the business follows, and it helps set a tone for decision making, client services and even vendor relationships. These are basically organizational morals, foundational standards in your business, to make sure you're staying on course. For example, one of our Core Values is to "do the right thing." It's very broad for a reason, because doing the right thing can mean so many things.

Our Core Values were developed together by the team, at the very beginning of our business, starting in 2009. I initially put out around seven or eight that I felt very strongly about. The team came back, through discussion and conversation, with additional values, and we worked on every value until we had team agreement. All of the Core Values are based on what we want to provide for our clients, the environment we want to create for clients and staff, and the direction we want to take the business to provide the best research-based training services. There was consensus around each core value, and agreement on why we want to include each value.

Our Core Values

1)	Trust in Teamwork

2)	Be Appreciative and Humble

3)	Do Whatever it Takes

4)	Delight the Client

5)	Do the Right Thing

6)	Be a Professional

7)	Continuously Learn and Evolve

8)	Be a Leader

9)	Bring Your Best Every Day

10)	Have Fun, a Sense of Humor, and Be Awesome

Ever since establishing the Core Values, we've been able to use them as a tool. I keep a blown-up copy of them in my office, to help me make decisions; the right decisions for the business. They have guided me in the right direction many times.

Once, just as I was about to leave for the day on Friday afternoon, one of our clients that I hadn't see in a while because she had been out of town, ran to the front desk, nearly in tears. There was no one else in the gym because it was closing time, so it was just me. Immediately, I could tell that she was obviously upset and distraught.

She was mad! She explained how she had told a staff member to put her account on a freeze since she was going to be away for a little while. But we had still billed her, and now, her account was overdrawn. It had resulted in several overdraft fees, and not being able to use her credit card while she was traveling on vacation.

We have a process for when a client needs to put a freeze on their account, and there's paperwork involved. Obviously, she hadn't completed that paperwork, which is why it happened. Instead, she told her trainer that she was leaving town, he told her he would take care of it, and he didn't. So, there I was, in a position to say, "Well, you didn't follow the procedure. You didn't fill out the paperwork. So, sorry." But, let's take a closer look. It wasn't her fault, and she's a valued client. I also didn't want to throw the trainer under the bus, because it was obviously just a mistake and oversight. I told her, "No problem, let me get you refunded right away." I wrote her a hard check that she could walk in with and cash at the bank. That way she also wouldn't have to wait for the credit card refund, which could take several days. We also refunded her overdraft fees.

Per our Agreement at the gym, I didn't have to refund her anything. She didn't follow policy, nor did the trainer. Technically, I could have reprimanded or fired the trainer. But that wouldn't have been the right thing to do. I knew that if I had been in her position, I would have wanted to have been taken care of. And, she walked out smiling, and we were both good by the end of it. She continued to be a faithful, happy client for several years, but all of that could have changed if we didn't "do the right thing."

If we hadn't had that moral compass, as a company, something to refer to as a foundation, to help us make good decisions, I think we would have lost that client, and she could have blasted us on Yelp, or some other review site. In this day and age, people are really quick to post negatively on review sites, so as a business owner you're at a disadvantage, since you're at the mercy of your customers. What if I had already left for the day when that client had come in. She may very well have blasted us on a review site, even though I wasn't aware of the situation, and didn't even really have a chance to do anything about. When that happens, and I see a really negative review, I look at it, and figure out how I can do the right thing - for that client and for the business. As a result, we enjoy a 5-star rating on Google, and 4.5 on Yelp.

Of all our Core Values, I think the hardest Core Value for me, as an individual, and us, as a team, is Core Value #9: "Bring Your Best Everyday". There are so many variables in life that come up; maybe you're having a bad day, maybe there's a death in the family. On those tough days, it's hard to bring your best, but you just have to get through the day and be the best you can on that day. Now, on the surface, you have to look like you're having a great day. Ultimately, it can help you to be focused on something positive, to get through difficult times, and the team is here to support each other.

It is business critical to build core values, write them down, and build every team effort and decision made, around them. These are not just one-off values that you jot down, put in a folder, and put away, never to be seen again. These are visited again, and again - sometimes daily. They need to be internalized within you and your staff, so you don't even really need to see them; you just feel them.

To have this foundation, a physical reminder of what you stand for as a business, builds trust in the team. It helps that team work together. We're going to be appreciative of what we have because there are people far less fortunate than us. We get to show up every day, do what we love to do, and be humble about it. It reminds us that sometimes there are things outside of the scope of our "job description," that we're just going to have to do. Do whatever it takes to get the job done. Sometimes that means mopping up a spill or accompanying a client to their car if it's dark outside.

Having core values is just going to be an overarching umbrella over every decision you make in your business. Without having something like these core values every single day you can be hit in the face with decisions that aren't clear without them. Having them, seeing them and practicing them isn't extra work. If anything, they make your life much easier, especially when it comes down to making good decisions for your company.

Andy Frisella, a well-known podcaster covering all topics related to being a business owner and manager, spends time talking about core values, including in relation to hiring and firing employees. He emphasized creating a positive culture in your business - a living, breathing culture that IS your company. Look at a company like Harley Davidson, he suggests. Here you have your typical "biker" client base, alongside a doctor, for example, and they have found common ground and humanity within the Harley culture. This culture comes from those core values, and what your company stands for. If you don't hire and fire by those core values, you'll lose that "X" factor that IS your company, and what it represents in the community.

These core values aren't just for you to know, understand, and live. Your entire team has to be engaged with them. The very first day that someone begins, or usually in the interview process, we go over our Mission Statement and our Core Values, and what it means to be a part of the business. This is what we stand on, it's our foundation. Once they become an employee, they see the Core Values and Mission Statement on the wall in the coach's office, we talk about it once a week in our Tuesday team meetings. Each week, we talk about one of the Core Values, or if someone is "giving props," or being noticed for following these Core Values, we make sure everybody knows about it.

For example, "Trust in Teamwork" is a good one. Someone at the team might give "props" to a coach for volunteering to take an extra shift because someone was sick, or otherwise couldn't make it to work. Team members know that other team members are there to take care of the clients, and to help each other. No one had to make those specific arrangements to cover a client's appointment - it just happens, organically, because this Core Value is in place, and supported.

The consistency of bringing this up regularly helps build the culture and reinforces these core values. In business, eventually problems will occur, and when they do occur, we work to solve them. Unfortunately, sometimes once we have the solution, we go back to our old ways, and the problem reoccurs over and over. We've created the Core Values to help solve problems and a guide to how to act inside the business. But, if we never go back to them, the problems keep coming up over and over. Weekly meetings help us avoid this.

I find that these core values carry outside of the gym, too. When any of our team members goes out into the public, he or she knows that they have to do the right thing. It's ingrained in our culture, and we carry it throughout our lives. Wearing our shirt or not, this is a community where people know who we are. You can't act out and act foolish in public, either. I think we all try to set that example for one another. That we represent the gym, inside the gym, and outside the facility. That we are ambassadors, in some ways. Our Core Values aren't just about how to act in the gym, they readily translate to our being a good human being and citizen.

When I meet with business owners who are trying to grow their business, I talk with them about

114

this aspect pretty early on in most of our conversations. I need to know, for example, if this is even on the radar for a business owner client. Do they understand the principle behind having core values, and if they do, what are they - let's take a look at them. Sometimes they have them defined and written out, but most of the time they don't. We advise that the core values that they have developed need to be in-front, and acted on, every day.

I recommend that the core values are built together, as a team, as early as possible when starting a new business, or when trying to re-establish a current business. If these core values are coming from the top-down, there's no buy-in, because the vast majority of the team doesn't feel like these belong to them, because, they don't. If you're trying to build a positive culture, then your team is going to help pass along your message, in the community and to the clients. The core values that you and your team develop need to reflect you, and your moral compass, as well as that of each team member. That buy-in is key to the success for creating a positive culture.

I think most people follow core values within themselves, regardless if they're on a piece of paper or not. A lot of these core values are consistent with just being a decent human being. But, the hard decisions, where having something like this in place, helps us make good decisions, decent decisions, and helps us do the right thing. They're not anything magical - this is what you do if you're a good human people, living your life on this earth - it's pretty basic.

Sometimes it's pretty obvious when a team member isn't up to the task of upholding our Core Values. At times, it just means having a chat, and at other times, it means that they need to work somewhere else. If their own core values are positive and strong, most of the time we can work with them, and learn something from each other. But it depends on the person. Sometimes it takes a while to find that perfect fit, and to find that perfect team for yourself.

Always look toward the long-term versus the short-term gain. People look for a magic fix all the time. But, the longer I'm in this game, the foundational things keep coming back over and over. Making the right decision. Having the right programs in place. Avoiding scam marketing tactics just to get people in the door. You never win in the long run. It's boring to say, but standing on those foundational principles, and sticking to positive core values, will keep you moving in the right direction.

Exercise

What are your personal core values?

_____

_____

_____

_____

_____

_____

_____

Which of these carries to your business?

_____

_____

_____

_____

_____

_____

_____

What core values are exclusive to your business?

_____

_____

_____

_____

_____

_____

_____

How and when will you review these core values with your team, and develop a team-written version?

_____

_____

_____

_____

_____

_____

_____

How will you ensure that your business core values become part of the culture of the business?

_____

_____

_____

_____

_____

"Your values create your internal compass that can navigate how you make decisions in your life. If you compromise your core values, you go nowhere."

Roy T. Bennett

Chapter 10

Leverage Tools

Back in 2009 when I was introduced to Infusionsoft, I didn't realize all the things that a piece of software could do to help manage and run a business. For example, automating daily tasks of running a business; from follow-ups, check-ins at the gym, daily summaries, weekly reports, and so forth. These are things that are redundant and can be automated, and there are, most likely, tools that you can leverage. These tools help you buy some time. Time that you can better spend working on your business.

You never get time back, right? People who know me understand that I will always "buy" time. By that, I mean that I will always invest in things that are going to save me my personal time, even if it's not

100% the same thing I would do. I may "buy" a mentor to shortcut a process, or a coach to solve a problem so I don't have to use my time to bang my head against the wall trying to figure something out. I may buy software that automates mundane processes in the business so that I can have my time back.

By doing that, I've been able to leverage myself multiple ways, and I'm actually able to do things that generate more revenue. When I'm not typing the same email, every day, five times a day, but instead create a campaign once, and it's got its own schedule, then I don't have to do it anymore. Then, I can use my time to generate revenue and cut expenses with automation.

A lot of business owners think that it's important to do everything they can themselves to save money, and that's not the right mentality to help you grow your business. Don't try to save money by spending your time. When I look at whether or not I'm going to invest in something, I look at the return on investment. So, let's just say that I see a service that will automate a task at the gym, and it costs $500 a month. At our current membership rates, all I need to do is sign-up two more people, and retain them for the entire year. That's how I make my decisions.

If something's going to help me, and just getting one more person is going to pay for the entire thing, and I can continue using that service or product after that person has moved on, I'll invest in it, because it makes a lot of sense. What's the return on investment? Is it simply time, so that I can turn around and generate more revenue? Am I going to make more money doing the things I need to do with my new free-time than it costs for this task to be done? If yes, then that's how I'm going to invest my money.

Instead of looking at how much money you might "save" by doing something yourself, look at it through a different lens. If you will make more money and get more time back in your day, then, that's the right decision to make.

Having a way to automate leads can be critical when it comes to leveraging tools to build your business. Tools can nurture leads through automation when that potential client isn't ready to buy right now. It sure would be nice if you could just open your door, and have people waiting in line to buy a membership. This does occasionally happen, maybe not a line of people out the door, but you'll get a small group showing up every once in a while.

More common is when someone drives past your building, they see your business, drive past it again, and this goes on. They may next be surfing on social media and see your ad pop up. Then they look up your website, maybe read a few blogs and see something they like, and fill out the contact form. That lead then goes into whatever system you have in place.

If you're responding manually, you'll spend hours and hours trying to get that client in the door.

With a tool like Infusionsoft, you set it up once, and it runs itself. In our case, that individual first receives an automated text thanking them for reaching out and provides a link for the consultation. If they don't respond to the text, a task is automatically forwarded to the front desk for that person to pick up the phone and reach out to the potential client. The system also has a feature to send out emails and voicemail broadcast to the new leads as different ways to communicate with the prospect.

If we still haven't signed up the client, we "drip" out a sequence of text messages, and after six or seven times of reaching out, typically they'll go into a sequence that includes a long-term nurture sequence. This sends out content, like healthy tips and recipes, the latest science of fitness, and over time, they may schedule their consultation. We've had people in the system being nurtured for two or three years before they come in.

The power of having automation is the power of having those long-term nurture sequences that can build a client relationship, long before the person is actually a client. If you're staying on their radar, and you're giving out valuable content, when the time comes, they're going to think of you first. For example, we can track a potential client in the lead system through the Infusionsoft dashboard, and every Tuesday in our Team Meeting, we go over every single person that has enrolled in a Trial Membership, as well as almost every client in the gym. The automated tools work only with thoughtful, personalized management of the lead system.

Our clients are paying us to hold them accountable, so that's on us. They want to feel like you care. There are some things Infusionsoft, or any other automated system, can't do. But we can still leverage automation to trigger phone calls and text messages. For instance, one of my favorite automated practices is if somebody hasn't been in for a week, they get an automatic voicemail from our Fitness Director (their phone never rings and the message is routed direct to voice mail) checking in, making sure everything is OK, and asking for a return phone call or text for an appointment. We never let anybody get more than seven days without being on our schedule. If they are on the schedule, and they don't show up, they get a call, immediately or that day. This is done through the program, Skipio. Between that program and Infusionsoft, you can get a great start into automating basic and advanced business functions.

I talk a lot about Infusionsoft, but I'm not a distributor. My favoring it and sharing it with you is strictly based on my first-hand knowledge of this important tool. It's a software that we have learned over time, and have it leveraged to the max in my businesses. There are several different softwares available on the market, however, since I'm familiar with Infusionsoft, let me give you some details that might help you understand the need for automation, costs, benefits and trouble-shooting. For us, for instance, Infusionsoft costs approximately $300/month, which includes email integration, which can be integrated with other tools like text automation, and with Zapier (third- party tool). Zapier is a software that can integrate thousands of different software together. Once something connects to Zapier, you can connect to pretty much anything you want. You can use it to create task notifications for your staff, generate invoices, create pipeline reports, automate leads into custom Facebook Audiences or generate reporting on your marketing efforts. You can move leads from your website into Infusionsoft, including taking payments. It's almost unlimited and is just bound to grow in functionality as the technology is developed.

I don't know if I'm a software junkie, but if I see a software, and I can see how I can use it, with the knowledge that the cost of the software can be covered quickly, I'll invest in it. My team has had to learn Infusionsoft, Zapier, WordPress, Skipio, Clickfunnels and other programs; they must learn them because we've integrated them into our business. I'm attracted to automation because I see it as something that will save me time. I always see the payoff of what any tool I buy can do for me.

This may change in a few years, but the way to communicate with clients today is through text message and Facebook messenger. Those messages are the way people communicate today.

Email is still a viable option as a backup. You might hear about the open rates of emails being 20-30%, but I think it's closer to 20%, and it might be that the emails are going straight to SPAM because of email providers protecting their users. With a text message, you can reach someone directly without a chance of SPAM filters.

Balance is the key here, because automation tools make it easy. However, if you send too much, or don't include meaningful, quality information, you might also aggravate a potential client. The best way to avoid that is to communicate with them in the opt-in form. Let them know you will be sending information, promotions, content and how often. If they're a client, they expect to be communicated with. But you have to move cautiously with leads and potential clients. In general, potential clients start to funnel into our lead conversion system by us connecting with them relatively quickly by email and text message, so they don't forget what they "opted-in" for.

For example, if someone is on our order form, and they don't close the sale within 15 minutes or so, we will nudge them with a text and/or email. We always, then, drive them back to that order form, pre-populated with anything they had started adding. These nudges are always personalized, with the person's name and what they were looking at. We also offer a wide variety of ways to pay for their purchase. We want to make it as easy as possible. I call this reducing the friction to a sale. If they don't initially respond, we send something for the next few days, approximately four times in the next three days. After that, it goes to phone calls. Most of the time these potential clients are signing up for the paid trial offer, and I recommend all gym owners start here.

Typically, 30 days or less, the trial offer is designed to let people visit, and try your product or service before they're ready to buy an annual package. It's similar to going on a test drive for a new car or trying out a movie streaming service at no cost for a month. The cost of a trail can range from as little as $7 up to $299, depending on your market and model. Our most successful price point is between $97-$147, which typically brings in a higher quality client. Since they are willing to spend about $100 for a 14-day trial, they tend to be more serious about their fitness program. They're a client for that entire time, and they're treated like a regular client, so they are welcomed immediately into our community.

Our entire team knows how to do this, and they know that the growth of the business depends on keeping current clients, and truly welcoming new, potential clients. We track people in this trial, in part with automated tools, so we reach out every few days, and we know exactly where they are within the trial. It runs like a machine, and it results in high conversion into permanent client status. I like the 14-day timeline because we know within two weeks whether or not client is going to stick around. If they come in at least three times a week, we can usually tell they are a "good fit" for the gym.

Everyone working at the gym is incentivized on memberships; the more members we have, the more money everybody makes. Having tools that streamline new membership campaigns maximizes everybody's potential to earn more.

Unfortunately, in the gym business, we've set up our own barriers. Many people have been burned with oppressive contracts, and they're afraid to come into gyms. They feel like they're a number and not a person. They don't feel like anyone cares about them. When they attended other gyms in the past, nobody talked to them. That's what people think of gyms and fitness businesses and that's where the industry is failing the general population. The industry's failure is evident by the increasing obesity rate. People aren't getting in better shape, they're getting in worse shape. The model that we run is more of a service-based, coaching model. Holding people accountable and supporting their goals and progress. Because this requires a lot of touch points, we leverage tools and automation to help us do that.

Automation can include sending handwritten birthday cards (using software) with gift cards or sending personalized gift baskets. Things like that can build relationship and show that you value your clients. You can then spend more time creating a positive environment for your clients and your staff, instead of sitting at your desk writing out birthday cards. The core message is still there - that the recipient matters, and you value their business and loyalty.

Another tool that is popular right now is using Chatbots. Chatbots on Facebook or your website can be incredibly valuable. In this day and age, people want a response, NOW! They don't want to put in an email and get a response in two to three days. Especially if it's just a basic question. Having basic chat options with question automation is a great idea, since that's how people want their information these days. If you go to any of our websites, you'll see a live chat box pop up. We use a program called OctaChat where there is a live person available that has been trained on all our websites and businesses. If they don't have the information, they get the contact information of the individual and we get them in our system and answer their question personally.

All of these systems have been integrated into our processes over time. A lot of the automated tools didn't even exist when we started the business. Or, the technology existed, but really didn't work well, or the return on investment wasn't there. We started the business with Infusionsoft within the first year of opening the gym. Other automation programs have been implemented just within the last year. If I'm working with a business client, who is looking for help and advice, I may recommend any or all of these products, as long as I think they have the capacity to understand the importance of using these tools. If, on the other hand, they're just struggling with getting leads, or opt-ins, then we start with simple strategies.

Many of these tools have been amazing for us. We saw a 12% increase in conversions when we introduced Live Chat. There was a 35% conversion increase from the "abandoned cart" sequencing. They are added to the abandoned cart sequence when they start the process to join the gym but do not complete the transaction. With the automated email, text and phone call process, we were able to convert that impressive percentage from those starts. We know, based on statistics to all ecommerce sites, that between 80-85% of consumers "abandon" their cart, so tackling this head-on brings us in a significant conversion percentage increase from our efforts. Leveraging these tools, and converting those leads, allows you to grow your business in ways that you can't do if you're working on your own, manually, trying to turn leads into customers. Tools like these are meant to serve a purpose. Remember that we use them when needed and they eventually lead to human interactions either in person or on the phone with a conversation.

Exercise

What types of tasks can be automated at your gym or business?

_____

_____

_____

_____

_____

_____

What is currently automated?

_____

_____

_____

_____

_____

_____

Which task can you automate within the next 30 days?

_____

_____

_____

_____

_____

_____

What software or program application do you need to invest in to implement basic automations?

_____

_____

_____

_____

_____

_____

"Automation is cost cutting by tightening the corners and not cutting them."

Haresh Sippy

Chapter 11

Learn How to Sell

I think I know why a lot of gym owners can't sell. A lot of them get into the fitness business because they want to help people; they want to change lives. They're technicians. They know how to train people, they know how to nurture them through a process, they know what it's going to take to help this person reach their potential. Deep in their core, they truly want to help this person.

The flipside to this is that, in order to provide that service, and sell that service to someone, they are taking money from them. They see that as "hurting" the person, by taking that money from them. The trainer may not even be in a position financially to be able to afford their own services, so there may be an unhealthy relationship with money taking place as well. When that happens, the trainer or gym owner doesn't feel like their services are worth paying for, or they feel that, accepting payment for their time and expertise, is not helping their client.

As a result, a couple of things happen. First, they discount their rates to an unsustainable amount. Or, they don't know how to sell, and constantly lose opportunities to make a living earning money for their services. Sometimes this is because that trainer doesn't understand the value of what they're bringing to the table. They have the potential to change somebody's life, to add quality years to their lifespan. That's worth money.

But, because the trainer is usually in great shape, working out comes naturally to them, and it's not hard for them, they tend to devalue what they're providing. Their client is struggling, and the trainer has a solution for them, and that's very valuable. I always say, "we're not selling cigarettes and booze to our clients, we're selling a lifestyle of health and fitness". What we're doing is life changing, and so it's very valuable. You must always remember that.

There are very few trainers that are good salespeople. But, they're out there. And, if you happen to have a trainer on staff who is also a good salesperson, that employee can be extremely valuable to you. That person can, almost literally, be your goldmine. This balance of skills means that the trainer has to be able to talk to the client on a technical level, they need to understand the training protocols, and they also can't be afraid of money. More commonly, you have a strict salesperson who knows nothing about training, or a trainer that knows nothing about sales. But, if you can put those two together, that's your MVP. When you find that combination in an employee, do your best to keep that person on your team.

Either way, the only way to stay in business is to sell your products or services for a profit. You have to generate revenue. You generate revenue by making sales. Now, I understand the difficulty. Early on, I wasn't good at sales, I didn't know how to sell. I didn't value what I was doing. But that changed when I started working with clients, seeing their results, and helping them change their lives. A light bulb went off, and I realized that what I was doing was pretty valuable. I also became very confident that our services would solve their problem.

Do you know your target audience? Are you tailoring your marketing message to your target market? All of your messages need to be in alignment with who you are trying to attract. From my experience, most of my gym owner clients are looking for the 30-55-year-old female that wants to get fit, lose fat and "tone up." The average age of clients at my gym, are 40-45-year-old females, so I know this market well. When I first start working with a gym owner, I ask them to tell me who they think their perfect client is. A lot of time, they don't know, and they stumble around a little, especially if they're a newer gym owner. There's nothing wrong with this; they just don't know, yet. How would they?

But, bottom line, to sell your service, you have to know who you're selling to. It might change over time. Maybe when you first opened, you thought you were going to have a younger clientele, but maybe that population just isn't in your area, and your clientele looks different than you thought they would. So, you have to make sure your selling, and your marketing match who your perfect clients actually are. If you like working with a population different than who you are reaching, then you have to target your message differently. Everything from the color of your imagery and advertising, to the language you use in your copy. It all has to speak to the brain of your perfect client, and they need to know you are offering something valuable to them. You also have to be able to speak to solving their problem, and how you can help.

Here's something you need to know about the fitness business. Only 16% of the adult population of the United States are members of a gym or fitness club. So, right away, the cards are stacked up against you - fully 84% of the population probably isn't interested in what you do. From there, you have to convince people to trust you and your process, without really knowing you. Now, if you are targeting the wrong audience, when you're already up against the selling/marketing wall, you will be up the creek, without a paddle.

If you are absolutely confident that you are going to provide someone a valuable result, selling becomes easy. At that point, you're not really selling. You're just explaining how you know you can help someone. You're not pushing anything, you're only showing that potential client what you will do to help them. Once you stop being confident in your product or services, you will start struggling in sales. If you don't feel good about what you're selling, it comes across in your presentation or pitch.

Most of us have a negative impression of a salesperson. My mental image, when I was first getting started, was that stereotypical used-car salesman, or a huckster. A greasy guy, coming in and looking for money, really sly, not trustworthy, and not honest. So, that was how I pictured myself, almost, when I first had to sell my products and services. That's a big turn off, and I didn't want to be seen that way.

When I started talking to real people, over and over again, and hearing their stories, things changed for me. I went to every sales meeting with a potential client, trying to get to know them, versus trying to sell them something. I would let them ask me what the pricing was and slowed the process down. From there, the sales came easy.

"Tell me about you. What's going on in your life?" If I could find the pain and where they were struggling, then I knew I could help them. When they handed me information that helped me see and understand that, then "selling" was really clear and easy. You offer a valuable service that this person, sitting across from you, is willing to pay money for. Maybe they want to pay you to hold them accountable. Maybe they want to pay you to show them how to lose thirty pounds. If you feel confident about how you can help, you just need to lay out the plan on how you're going to hold that person accountable or help them lose weight. The service then sells itself.

Instead of thinking of sales as a pitch, think of it as a conversation - a dialogue. The ultimate salesperson is a problem solver. Find the problem that you can help with and get paid for that. Problem solved, with money in your pocket. Part of what you need is to be sure that your message is different from what's already out there in the marketplace. If what you're offering is the same thing that's offered down the street, the client is hearing the same message and seeing that you're not offering anything different. When that happens, between same or identical services, the client will almost always go with the cheaper alternative.

But maybe you're actually offering something completely different than the other gyms. Maybe your workouts are high-intensity, or maybe your nutrition plan is ketogenic, or you hold them accountable by a specific process that nobody else does. If you're trying to sell a message that sounds identical to the prospect as everyone else, then you're not going to make any sales, unless you're the cheapest option out there, which is usually not sustainable. You have to sell your message, and you have to make sure your message reflects how you're different, and how you're better. How do you do this? How do you make sure that your message matches your business?

We actually learned this from a man named Todd Brown, who is someone I really look up to. I heard him speak at an event, and his message really resonated. I approached Todd after the seminar and hired him as a consultant, because I knew I needed to understand, completely, what he was suggesting. I understood it on a surface level, but I wanted to go deep and make sure that I internalized this. This was one of those times that I made a huge investment and never looked back. Todd is a well-known, business guru, and his fee reflected that. But even my dad, standing next to me, who is also a consultant, knew that I had to hire Todd immediately to fully understand this philosophy and way of doing business.

My Dad, our Project Manager, and I, flew to Florida to meet with Todd. We stayed in a cheap hotel after arriving at around 10 p.m., woke up, had our pot of coffee, and showed up at 6:30 a.m. for our meeting. We just got to talking. One hour led to two, we kept going. Now, six hours in, and I'm looking at Todd thinking that this is the best investment I have ever made in my life - this guy is a genius. And I used everything that he taught us in every single marketing campaign, moving forward. I would not trade that five-figure fee for anything. I got every, single penny back, and then-some. I still have the notes from that meeting posted in my office.

Todd's strategies include the "unique mechanism for change." In other words, what is the one thing, the unique mechanism for change, that a prospect can only find at your gym. You must give people the reason to go see you versus everyone else. When they look at your product and service, they need to see something that is proprietary to you. It could be the same thing that the gym down the street is offering, for example, a specific fitness program. But you call it something different. So, instead of saying that you offer "fitness," you offer a "metabolic burn method." Our nutrition plan is the "lean body formula." We hold clients accountable through a "proactive accountability technique." This is all packed in a "tri-pillar blueprint" that prospects see as a graphic with these three components, and it sets us apart.

That client might be a current member at another gym, and think they're not getting results because "Joe's Gym" doesn't offer a "proactive accountability technique," or a "lean body formula," or the "metabolic burn method." These are just unique ways of referring to accountability, nutrition and fitness methodology, and in a way that sets you apart, because your technique is different. It's not just a name, it's a different program, a more specific offering that you have than your competitors down the street. Nobody else offers it, because you created it. You named it. You don't necessarily have to reinvent what you're doing that's already unique, but you do have to give it a unique name that can only be found at your facility.

To give you an idea of how well this worked for us, that initial meeting with Todd was in early 2017. We instituted everything he taught us by May of that year. We had our best campaign we had ever run, bringing in almost $170,000 in revenue just that month. The return on my investment of paying Todd as much as I did, was amazing. Having him as a mentor really helped us tie-up our sales pitch, so that it made it easy to sell. So, part of learning to sell is learning WHAT to sell, and how to attach a meaningful message to what you're selling. If you are selling a unique product or service, selling is easier.

You'll see huge corporations doing this all the time. Pay attention to marketing campaigns of fitness companies, or even just TV commercials for all sorts of products from shampoo to vacuum cleaners. They use "proprietary" names for things that everyone else is doing, but because it has a unique name on it, even if there's absolutely no science or true uniqueness behind it, it seems that they're offering something unique.

Orange Theory, for example, put their flag into the ground and decided to own the "Orange Zone," (their name for the "fat-burning" heart rate zone) which has been well-established for decades as the best heart rate range to burn-fat. But, by giving it a name, now it's a "unique" twist on fitness that really isn't unique at all. Heart-rate monitors existed long before there was Orange Theory. The 80% max heart-rate zone has been around forever. But, they "created" this principle around it, and named it. Someone across the street could be doing the same thing, but they don't have the "Orange Zone" so they just "can't possibly get the same results." It's the genius of marketing and resulted in massive growth as a franchise.

So, you either take something that isn't really new, and you put a new name on it, as well as a marketing spin, and you package it as unique. Or, you truly create something from scratch, something new, like CrossFit, and package it that way. That second option is obviously more difficult and may or may not be something you want to do. But it is an option that can help you sell something truly unique.

The greatest companies are not the ones that offer the greatest products or services; the greatest companies are the ones that excel at marketing and sales. Think about the Rock and Roll industry. Think about the best guitar player in the world. Think about the best vocalist in the world. Now, you and I may have different opinions on this, but think about the artists that have been around for decades, and still sell out huge arenas, Bon Jovi, Bruce Springsteen, the Rolling Stones, for example. Now, is Jon Bon Jovi the best vocalist? Is he the best guitar player in the band, or in Rock and Roll? Maybe, or maybe not. But Jon Bon Jovi is business savvy, he knows how to market himself, his band, and the music. These artists sell out shows, months in advance, not because they're the best musicians, they're the best marketers of their business. They sell the performance with confidence. They have been doing it for decades without a break, creating an audience and fan base

So, what makes someone stand out as a great salesperson in the gym business? There are some basic personality characteristics and skills. First and foremost, would be the speed to contact; how quickly do you answer an email, text message, online form, phone call? This is key to getting conversions because it shows that you're attentive, and you're responding shortly after the potential client has reached out, so the lead is still "hot." The quicker you can get back to them, the better. People lose interest, and move onto the next thing, if you don't respond almost instantly.

I needed work done on my garage door and went to Angie's List. Once I filled out the contact info and what I was looking for, I was forwarded a list of five contractors who could do the job. So, I started reading the reviews of the first one to get an idea of what his clients thought of him. Before I finished the second review my phone rang, and it was that contractor saying he had been notified that I was interested in getting some work done on my garage. I hired him because he reached out and was fast. He didn't wait, and neither should you. Be like that guy.

Secondly, in this day and age, it is important to be honest; having an honest sales pitch is critical. This almost feels like an oxymoron - honest salesperson. These two words don't have to conflict with each other. If you're sitting across the table from a potential client, and they feel like you genuinely care about their results, it helps the sales process. There are all sorts of techniques during that sales pitch, like Neuro-Linguistic Programming (NLP) or using body language and brain science to close the deal, but back to basics, honesty, and truly caring about somebody, is the best way, in my opinion, to close a sale. Otherwise, we're just manipulating someone into a sale, and that doesn't feel like a good way to start a long-term client relationship, to me.

Another thing to consider is your price. If you are constantly discounting your price, just to get customers in the door, what is it telling your community about how you value your own services? In the fitness industry I find that if a potential client is going to be a good, long-term member, they will demonstrate that commitment just by signing-on to a higher-priced program than maybe you're used to offering. When you have a trial offer, for example, I suggest that you have an offer for a paid trial, not a free trial.

People who sign-up for "free" stuff aren't really committed and may not even show up because they have nothing to lose. You've just given away that space in your gym to someone who will, most likely, never convert to a lifelong client. People who have money on the line, even if it's just $97 for 14-days, they are more likely to show up. They'll take advantage of the offer. I'm a 100% believer in the notion that, if someone puts more money down, they are going to show up, and be more committed. Every single time.

Be true to yourself, be honest, understand you have something very valuable to provide and what you do does change lives. Build your confidence by continuously creating great results for your clients and know without a shadow of a doubt that your product or service will solve your client's problems and you will be unstoppable.

Exercise

Who's the strongest natural salesperson on your team? What makes them a good salesperson?

_____

_____

_____

_____

_____

_____

What services are you providing now that you can "re-package" as a proprietary service?

_____

_____

_____

_____

_____

_____

How can you brand yourself as unique from a competitor?

_____

_____

_____

_____

_____

"Pretend that every single person you meet has a sign around his or her neck that says, 'Make me feel important.' Not only will you succeed in sales, you will succeed in life."

Mary Kay Ash

Thank you for reading my book!

Whew! I know that was a lot to take in. Thank you for spending your time with me. I hope you found Built to Grow valuable and that you will share this book with another gym owner that needs to hear the messages written on the pages of this book.

I am here to help you grow your business. I have tools available right now that can help you create a profitable and sustainable business. Our GPS product has been a valuable tool that our clients have been leveraging with great success. I wrote about GPS in Chapter 3, and if you'd like to start using the GPS to grow your business you can visit our website: www.profitgps.net to get started with it right away.

I am on a mission to help as many gym owners as I can, change the trajectory of their businesses and lives and I want to help you too.

You've read the book, go ALL-IN and schedule a Breakthrough Call with me today to grow your business…

www.pfmarketingsolutions.com/call

Keep Changing Lives!

Tim Lyons

50395196R00093

Made in the USA
Columbia, SC
06 February 2019